pretty

girl

in

crimson

rose

(8)

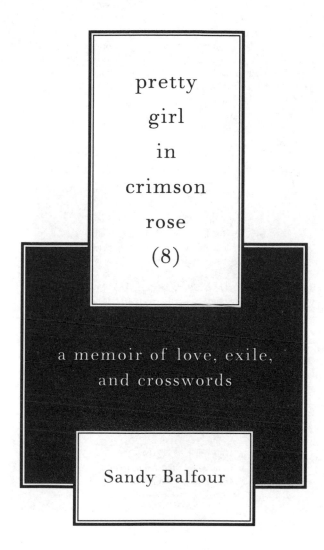

pretty
girl
in
crimson
rose
(8)

a memoir of love, exile,
and crosswords

Sandy Balfour

JEREMY P. TARCHER/PUTNAM

a member of Penguin Putnam Inc.

New York

Most Tarcher/Putnam books are available at special quantity discounts for bulk purchase for sales promotions, premiums, fund-raising, and educational needs. Special books or book excerpts also can be created to fit specific needs. For details, write Putnam Special Markets, 375 Hudson Street, New York, NY 10014.

Jeremy P. Tarcher/Putnam
a member of
Penguin Putnam Inc.
375 Hudson Street
New York, NY 10014
www.penguinputnam.com

Library of Congress Cataloging-in-Publication Data

Balfour, Sandy, date.
Pretty girl in crimson rose (8) : a memoir of love, exile, and crosswords / by Sandy Balfour.
    p.   cm.
ISBN 1-58542-198-7
1. Balfour, Sandy, date.   2. Television journalists—South Africa—Biography.   3. Crossword puzzles.
I. Title: Pretty girl in crimson rose (eight).   II. Title.
PN5476.B33A3   2003   2002032159
        070.92—dc21

Printed in the United States of America
1   3   5   7   9   10   8   6   4   2

This book is printed on acid-free paper. ∞

Book design by Stephanie Huntwork

for my girlfriend

Though he is a person to whom things do not happen,

perhaps they may when he is on the other side.

FROM *THE UNSTRUNG HARP* BY EDWARD GOREY

contents

Part Two

the birth of an englishman

Part Three

a biographical puzzle

prologue

I remember cities by their skylines at night.

Below the green crest of Primrose Hill, London is a sparkling sprawl. The buildings seem to be talking to one another, like parents over the heads of their wayward children. On a clear winter's night you can see all the way across the city to Crystal Palace, where the flashing lights on the radio tower answer those on the skyscrapers of Canary Wharf. Perhaps it is a conversation in a bus queue; you can listen in if you want.

Manhattan by contrast is too loud to hear. I was never so alone as when I walked across the Brooklyn Bridge just before dawn, to be swallowed whole by the canyons.

And I remember once flying into Kai Tak, in Hong Kong. There was a powerful wind as we broke through the cloud cover and swept in below the high-rise buildings of Kowloon. From my window seat I watched a woman hang out her washing in silhouette against the window of her apartment. I wanted to help her, to hold her sheet's flapping corner while she took the peg from between her teeth.

A cityscape doesn't have to be tall to linger in the memory. From the Havana Libre the broad sweep of the Malecón reaches around to the harbor entrance. Low-wattage lights cast soft shadows on the peeling stucco façades. The last time I was there I made a deal with a moneychanger sitting on the rocks. He wore ersatz Ray-Bans and ersatz Levi's, and since I have no Spanish, we got by in ersatz German. We had to read the numbers on the faded banknotes by moonlight, while behind us the Florida Straits pounded the seawall. I remember the modest skyline as a cardboard-cutout movie set. I expected Gary Cooper to appear and rid the town of people like me, once and for all.

Then there is Johannesburg, the place where I was born.

Johannesburg is a city on a hill, built on the "white water ridge," the Witwatersrand, where the settlers first found gold toward the end of the nineteenth century. You can see it from miles around.

On a particular night in the southern winter of 2000, a friend and I sit looking at the city's impressive and inviting skyline. We have an unusual vantage point, because on a whim we have driven to the Top Star drive-in cinema south of the city. The drive-in is one of Johannesburg's landmarks. It has been built on top of a mine dump, one of many eyesores that line the southern edge of the city. The mine dumps are steep, and by day they are a pale yellow color. But by night all that disappears, and they stand as pools of darkness in a streetlit world

It is late, and there is nobody about, but my friend and I have a sense of being illicit. We had to remove a barrier to get in and we drove up the steep access road with the car lights turned off. We laugh to find ourselves whispering. Our voices are, in any case, swallowed by a chill wind blowing from the south. It carries the smell of the coal fires of Soweto.

To escape the wind, we pick our way through razor wire and climb the metal-and-wood frame of the movie screen. We sit with our backs to it, facing north, toward the city.

Individual buildings hold memories. There we did a piece to camera for a CNN film. There I negotiated football rights with a man subsequently jailed for stealing the money I had paid him. There I fell in love. There is the building I smashed into when a drunk driver's car hit mine as he sped through a red light. I fainted face down in the pool of his blood that dripped via my windscreen onto the tarmac.

Further north, in the tree-lined suburbs near Zoo Lake, my uncle lives in the house my grandfather bought. I remember Easter egg hunts in the garden and the early frost on the lawn.

To the east the skyline flattens out. Beyond the rugby stadium at Ellis Park it quickly gives way to the poorer suburbs of Bezuidenhout Valley. Farther south are the small hills of Kensington, which is where I was born.

"I've come full circle," I say, pointing in the general direction of Kensington. "I was born there, in the Marymount Maternity Hospital."

"Like a good Catholic," she says.

"Well, Catholic anyway."

My friend makes no response. It's an old joke, and in any case she appears lost in her own thoughts, wondering, perhaps, why she has chosen to leave England and live in a place like Johannesburg. At other times she has spoken of the narrowness of England, of the way it defines her. "I can't choose who to be," she once said, "when I'm at home."

She and I know each other well enough to sit in amicable silence and watch the lights. Downtown Johannesburg dies at night; there are few pedestrians, and fewer cars. One particular building in the middle of town grabs my attention. A surprising number of illuminated windows are arranged regularly like the squares on a crossword puzzle. If I start on the tenth floor, I can get a nine-letter word for one down and another for one across. I fill in "Marymount" and "Maternity," and wonder what I am going to do about "Hospital." Perhaps it will be easier if I call it a "clinic"? It bothers me that there are only enough lights on for a four-letter word at 2 down. "Rate," I decide arbitrarily. In that case 2 across—although in a real 15 x 15 puzzle it would be 7 or 8 across—is a six-letter word beginning T blank T. "Six letters," I say, "T blank T."

As it happens, my friend knows how to do crossword puzzles. She is English, after all, and went to an impressively expensive school in the Home Counties. Her father has a gratifying number of initials after his name, and her mother has worked for many years on the national newspapers. Although football is her passion, she understands the rules of cricket. It would be surprising if she did not know how to do crosswords.

"What are you on about?" she asks.

"That building there," I say, "to the right of the Carlton, and back a bit. It looks like a crossword puzzle." With much pointing I show her the particular building and explain why I have filled in the first two words. I do not need to explain to her about "checked" and unchecked letters. She already knows that in any crossword the checked letters are those that are shared with another word.

Just then a light goes out.

"Hah!" I say. "It's five letters now. Five letters, T blank T."

"That's easy," she replies. "Totti."

"'Totty'? I'm not having a word like 'totty' in my puzzle. I read the *Guardian*, for heaven's sake."

This is code for a sort of pseudo-new man, the kind who may or may not like "totty" in his newspaper, but who certainly won't admit it if he does.

"And anyway," I add, "the Y is only going to give us trouble when we find something for three down. I mean what's that? Five letters again, and it's M blank Y."

I am really quite passionate about this, and my voice rises until I realize that my friend is looking at me in the way people do before they send for the men in white coats.

"I was talking about the Italian footballer," she says coldly. "Totti, with an I."

"Oh. Well, you can't have that either," I reply. "Not enough people know who he is. I mean, how would you clue it? What's the definition going to be? Five letters. 'Italian striker gets the bird, we hear'? No, we need something better than that."

"Well then," she says, "you find your own word."

I experiment in my head. Total? Tithe? Titan?

"It's not a real puzzle," my friend says. "You do know that, don't you? It only exists in your head."

Somewhere far off, a police siren sounds.

"Can I ask you a question?" she says, and then she pauses. "Like, how did you get this way?"

"It's a long story," I say.

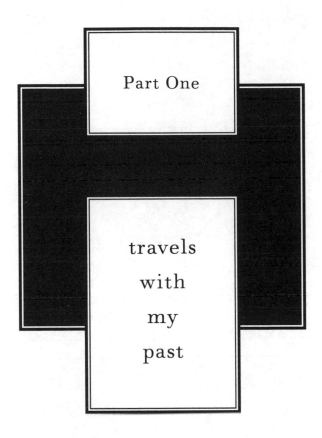

Part One

travels

with

my

past

maps
and
dreams

Let me take you back to December 1983.

My girlfriend and I leave South Africa at Beit Bridge, cross-ing the Limpopo River into Zimbabwe. Since early childhood I had thought of the Limpopo as described by Rudyard Kipling in his *Just So Stories*, as "grey, green and greasy." But now the whole subcontinent is in the grip of a terrible drought, and the river contains barely a trickle of water.

Picture, therefore, a brown bridge over a brown river set in a brown landscape. A brown soldier in a brown uniform inspects our papers. We wear bright colors and carry rucksacks.

"Where are you going?" he asks.

"London."

"In England," my girlfriend adds helpfully.

"That's nice," he says turning my papers over in his hand.

He puts them to one side and looks at me expectantly. "Do you have some cigarettes?" he asks.

"I don't smoke," I reply.

"That's not what I asked."

He is right. It is not what he asked. As it happens, I do have a pack of cigarettes for just such an occasion. I reach into my bag to find them, but something in the border guard's expression tells me that things are not that simple.

"You can give me money," he says, catching my eye.

I hand him some money.

My girlfriend looks studiously at the riverbed below us.

"How far is it to Harare?" I ask.

"If you're going to London," he replies, "what does it matter how far Harare is?"

It is just my luck to get a border guard with a degree in philosophy.

At this point in my life I have no knowledge of crosswords.

I am twenty-one years old.

On December 9, 1983, my girlfriend and I leave Cape Town to travel to London. Our plan is to hitchhike. My plan is never to return; her plan is to spend six months traveling, another six months earning some money in London, and then to return to South Africa. We have, in effect, given ourselves twelve months.

This obvious fault line in our relationship is not mentioned.

There is an assumption that things change.

There is an unspoken assumption that twelve months will just about do it.

I am not entirely comfortable with this assumption.

In preparation for the trip we have practiced hitchhiking. Two weekends previously we made the seventy-mile trip from Cape Town to Betty's Bay to meet a man who we had heard had just driven through Africa on a motorcycle. Perhaps, we think, he can give us some pointers. Perhaps he can tell us what to look for.

We hold up our thumbs, as though testing the wind. Betty's Bay is a resort-wannabe, an area of empty plots and holiday homes near the southern tip of Africa. When we get there a wind is whipping up the dunes, and white horses dance on the blue waters of the ocean. The Indian and Atlantic oceans "meet" somewhere near here. There is occasional debate about where exactly the dividing line is. Betty's Bay is west of Cape Agulhas but east of Cape Point and therefore falls into the disputed area. On this particular morning the sea is gloriously blue. The sun sparkles off the spray, and the coastal-range mountains gleam in clean afternoon light.

We arrive there late on a Saturday. The house of the man who has driven through Africa on a motorcycle is five miles inland, set at the end of a sandy track through a gray-green *fynbos*[1] landscape.

It turns out, however, that he is not there. It turns out that we have the wrong house altogether. It is too late to get back.

We spend the night huddled on the sagging *stoep* of a small hut several miles from anywhere. In the morning we eat sardines with tinned peaches. It is all we have. We had expected our traveler to feed us. My girlfriend is depressed, but it turns out that this is excellent training for what is to come.

DISSOLVE TO:

A ramshackle hut far from anywhere. Two young people sit on a stoep. Above them the roof sags beneath the weight of its history. Between them are two open tins. The tins appear to have been opened with a blunt axe by an ape. As the scene fades in, the young man scoops out a mangled sardine, sandwiches it between two slices of peach, and pops it in his mouth.

YOUNG MAN *(with his mouth full)*: You should try some.

YOUNG WOMAN: You think? It looks disgusting.

YOUNG MAN: All the great recipes have unlikely combinations. *(He takes another slice of peach.)* I mean there are millions of examples. *(Warming to his theme.)* Take salmon and cream cheese. Take duck and orange. Who'd have thought it?

YOUNG WOMAN: You could say the same of us.

YOUNG MAN: Yeah. *(Pause.)* So which am I, the duck or the orange?

(Long pause.)

YOUNG WOMAN: Well, I'm the peach.

I had made the decision to leave South Africa a year previously, when I graduated from university and received yet another set of call-up papers to the South African army.

But then I was able to put off the call-up for twelve months by taking a teaching job in one of Cape Town's coloured areas.

I was interviewed for the job.

For the interview I travel to the Department of the Interior (Coloured Affairs), in Wynberg. The administration of apartheid has given rise to many names, and over the years "Coloured Education" has fallen under the authority of a variety of government departments. It has only recently come under the authority of the Department of the Interior (Coloured Affairs). It is housed in a low brick building behind the train station. I am shown through to a bare room. At a desk are two white men. They have uniform moustaches and wear gray suits. They look miserable. One of them is smoking Peter Stuyvesant cigarettes. In South Africa at the time, Peter Stuyvesant runs advertisements that speak of a rich and varied jet-set world. We all know it. It is on all the magazine covers and in all the cinemas. It is a collage of sailing and skiing, of blond women and champagne. The world of the Peter Stuyvesant advertisements is a long, long way from the Department of the Interior (Coloured Affairs), in Wynberg.

The interview does not take long.

"So you want to teach?" one man asks.

I nod.

"Why?"

I make a pathetic attempt at humor. "Actually I just want a Coloured Affair," I say.

Silence.

"Mitchell's Plain, hey?" The man taps a pencil against his moustache. "Okay, you've got the job."

"That's it? That's the interview?"

"*Ja.* We just wants to be sure you's not a hippie."

"And am I?" I ask.

"No."

"Oh."

It is only in retrospect that I realize how the language of apartheid lends itself to crosswords. It is riddled with double and triple meanings. Plural affairs. Separate development. Total onslaught. Apartheid itself is an unlikely anagram. In 2002, for example, the *Independent* carried this clue: "Demolition of apartheid featured in list of successes (3,6)."*

A good crossword will be riddled with double and triple meanings. In a good puzzle, each clue should present itself as a mini-mystery. It is the setter who creates the mystery, and the mystery has two parts. One part of it is to find the solution. The other part is to find the connection between the "surface" meaning of the clue and the hidden meaning or answer. There must, in a good clue, be "good surface." That is to say, the clue must read easily and mean something. But the surface must also be misleading.

In almost all crossword clues, either the first or the last part

---

*HIT PARADE. By Phi, June 13, 2002.

of the clue will be synonymous with, or at least interchangeable with, or representative of, the solution. The balance of the clue is made of words, phrases, and meanings that make up the constituent parts of the solution. Take, for example, "Archer triumphant as storyteller (11)." Since the clue appeared in a British newspaper at the time that he was much in the news, we might expect it to refer to that well-known writer, Jeffrey, Lord Archer. He, after all, has enjoyed great commercial success through his writing, and he is famously something of a storyteller. The clue would seem to be about him. But it's not. The "surface" meaning is about him. The actual meaning is something altogether different.

In this example the answer is an eleven-letter word for "storyteller." The constituent parts are "bulls" and "hitter," which pertain to what triumphant archers do. They hit the bulls on the targets. When we put the two together, we get "bullshitter," a word that, in certain circumstances, might be used interchangeably with "storyteller."

When discussing Lord Archer, for example.

I loved teaching. I don't think I was very good at it, but I loved the ordered chaos of the classroom, the way a single word or thought could trigger ten or fifteen different responses. We had, of course, very little to work with. There were a blackboard and chalk, and some of the students in some of my classes had textbooks. But the school itself was newly built, and its classrooms were big enough, and light enough.

Armed with the knowledge that I was leaving, that I would not have to harvest the consequences of my bad teaching practice, I was able to take risks, and to teach without thought to discipline. My classes were disorderly, but fun. I was teaching, of all things, accountancy. I think it is fair to say I stretched the definition of "accountancy" beyond that set out in the textbooks we did have. In my world, accountancy incorporated Shakespeare and the novels of Jane Austen, politics and sport. In South Africa at that time, politics and sport were never very far apart. From time to time the Headmaster would reprimand me in his office. "We are teachers, not politicians," he would say. "We cannot help the children by filling their heads with ideas."

This was politics with a large and a small P. One day two boys came into class carrying a cane. They made pretense of threatening to hit another student. Filled with missionary zeal, I confiscated the cane and broke it into several pieces. I remember making an impassioned case against corporal punishment. I remember the way the boys in the back row giggled. I remember the girl in the front row who told me I would regret this. "They'll only get worse," she said.

The next day there was another cane, a little thicker this time, with less "swish." I duly confiscated it, and broke it into several pieces.

A third day . . . a third cane . . . a third speech.

In the staff room that lunchtime, two of my colleagues were making themselves a cup of tea. "If I ever find the little bastard who stole my cane," said the one with the moustache, "I'll kill him."

"You also?" said the other. "These fucking kids have no respect."

During that year as a teacher I engaged with my students, spent my weekends climbing mountains, and prepared to leave. That there was a conflict between any of these pursuits occurred to me only later.

And 1983 was a great year to be in Cape Town, in Mitchell's Plain. It was the year the United Democratic Front was launched. The arrival of the UDF promised the beginning of the end for apartheid. I hired a bus and took my students to the launch rally.

In 1983 there was a sense of things moving. The subsequent clampdown had not yet happened. The state of emergency had not been declared. Troops were not yet, by and large, occupying the townships. When the former prime minister, John Vorster, died, we had a *Vossie's gevrek!* (Vorster's dead!) party on Llandudno Beach outside Cape Town. Anything seemed possible.

It seemed perfectly possible, for example, to discard the life I had and to hitchhike to England. It seemed perfectly possible to be someone else.

In anticipation of this, I gave away everything I owned except for my rucksack, sleeping bag, tent and stove, and, of course, a wad of travelers' checks.

My girlfriend and I looked at maps, and bought rain ponchos.
My father wondered if I was not being a little dramatic.

I was being a little dramatic.

My father has himself made this journey, albeit going the other way. He grew up in Edinburgh and, like thousands of other children, was sent to the colonies after the outbreak of the Second World War. He was thirteen and presumably had few possessions to part with. Along with a sister and a brother, he made the hazardous trip by ship through the north Atlantic to Cape Town. Other ships full of children were less fortunate, and sank with all hands. In Cape Town an aunt put him on a train to boarding school in Grahamstown, where he spent the next four years. Since the war was not yet over, he then joined the South African army and spent some time fighting in North Africa and Italy. When he was demobbed they sent him "back," not to Edinburgh but to South Africa. He enrolled at the university in Johannesburg. Only once he had graduated, fully ten years after he first boarded that ship on the Clyde, did he finally make it back "home." His younger brother, who was three in 1939, didn't recognize him. "I remembered a boy," my uncle once told me, "not this man who I now found standing at the door. He was my brother, and I didn't know who he was."

In Cape Town in 1983, I find this process of preparing to leave very difficult. Ostensibly I am doing it for "political" reasons, in the sense that I am avoiding being conscripted into the apartheid army. But the truth is also that I want to go. I have a sense of a bigger world out there, a world where ideas have greater currency, and where words mean more. I am not sure what this means, and these thoughts are difficult to articulate. But I am certain that I want to move on, to be somewhere else. I can't, as my friend put it, choose who to be in South Africa. Over the final few months I become withdrawn and moody. I make lists of what I have to take. The more I give away, the shorter the list becomes.

By December I have only a desire to be on the move. I have cut myself off from friends and family. I have discarded my past. It feels like a kind of death. All that is left is my self.

I am not sure it is enough.

two

hearts

I don't know when I first came across a crossword puzzle. I do know when I first had the rules explained to me, but that was much later. I know also that when, finally, I became interested in them, I was predisposed to like them. In some way my childhood had prepared me for this, had prepared me to understand the point of a game which is essentially solitary, but which connects you to your peers.

My parents did not teach me the rules of crosswords, but they did teach me about games. "You need," they said, "to be open to the possibilities that the game presents." What my parents taught me about games is that the rules are only the beginning.

What happens after that is up to you.

.　.　.

I grew up in the sixties and seventies, in the time before South Africa had a television service. South Africa started test-broadcasting television in 1975, when I was thirteen. A "full" service began in 1976, but my parents acquired a television set only many years after I left home. I have memories of being marched down the road to the neighbor's house to watch *Civilisation* and *The World at War*. It was only in 1989 that my girlfriend and I bought our first set. By then we were living in a council flat at the Elephant and Castle in London, a few light-years away from my childhood.

In the absence of television, we had to find other ways to fill the evenings. My parents are middle-class white South Africans of the wartime generation. While my father did his service in North Africa and Italy, my mother would have knitted socks for the troops. It follows therefore that in the evenings at home we read books, and played bridge and chess. It was excellent training for a kind of old-fashioned Englishness.

It is not, perhaps, surprising that after living almost half my life in England, I now regard myself as English. From time to time it is necessary to nod politely to my South African roots, but these are small courtesies. I am not alone in thinking this. Americans, for example, think of me as English, as do Congolese rebels and Ghanaian cocoa farmers.

But English people do not regard me as English. My recalcitrant accent makes this impossible for them, as does my tendency to regard all sports as contact sports. To English people the defining point is not where I live, nor what values I have, but where I was born. Since I was not born in England, I will always be an immigrant, a foreigner. What this means is not that I behave badly, or have disturbing personal habits, but that I am unpredictable. I know them, but they do not know me.

I quite like this. There is comfort in otherness.

But it is only a partial otherness. In some respects I am "as English as the next man."

Take, for example, Jeremy Paxman's book *The English*. Paxman is a journalist and broadcaster of great distinction. His book was prompted by the moves within the United Kingdom to various forms of "devolution" of political power from the national parliament at Westminster. This devolution was, inevitably, accompanied by a nationalist rhetoric in both Scotland and Wales. Many began to ask whether or not there should be a similar rise in this kind of identity politics in England. But doubts were expressed as to whether or not the English really had any coherent sense of their own identity. Paxman therefore opens the book with a discussion of a time when he believes the English knew who they were. This is the time during and just after the Second World War. It is the time when David Lean made *Brief Encounter*, a touching exploration of a certain kind of repressed English sexuality. The film stars Trevor Howard and Celia Johnson as a couple desperately in love, but—since they are both married to other people—unable to consummate their budding relationship. Paxman writes of Celia Johnson's husband that he is the sort of man "to whom sympathy is the suggestion that they do the crossword together." He means this pejoratively.

I was deeply moved by this line because I am just that sort of man. I am the sort of man to whom it is sympathetic to do the crossword together.

I wonder what this says about me.

Trevor Howard and Celia Johnson never get it together in *Brief Encounter*. Trevor Howard, in preference to making love with Celia, flees to South Africa, where he is to tend to the sick. Quite what the sick of South Africa have done to deserve such attention is not discussed. That South Africa is a safe distance from the turbulent emotions of the Home Counties of England is taken as read.

Even now this amuses me more than I can say.

South Africa never struck me as a place of safety.

My father has a flair for bridge, and for the dramatic. To this day, under the right circumstances, he will tell an exaggerated but nonetheless entertaining version of the story of how he and my mother met at a bridge club in the fifties.

I say "under the right circumstances" because my father is a very shy man, and he needs social situations to have a degree of formality in order to flourish. For more than fifty years, contract bridge has provided him the necessary degree of formality.

Within bridge there are rules and conventions, but there is also space for the moment of improvisational genius, for the instinctive play and the hunch bid. The game provides people like my father with an arena in which a certain kind of understated aggression is allowed, or even desirable.

My father thrives in this sort of environment. Compared with him, my mother, my sister, and I are weak players, and over the years he has become accustomed to playing with a certain disregard for the normal conventions. He is accustomed, for example, to opening with a bid of four spades without first having looked at his cards. In bridge the point is for two players partnering each other to use a complex set of bidding codes to arrive at a "contract" for how many tricks they will make. Neither has seen the other's cards, nor the cards of the opposing players. The bidding conventions are therefore a way of telling your partner what kind of cards you have in your hand. It also tells your opponents. My father is of the view that our opponents will find it very difficult to play against someone who opens four spades without first looking at his cards. He seems to care less that I find it virtually impossible to play *with* someone who bids four spades without looking at his cards.

I play with my father against my mother and my sister.

My sister claims she always played with my father, and that she bore this cross without complaint. I asked my father about it and he said, "Oh, nonsense. It was always boys against girls." I suspect, of course, that the truth is "a bit of both." Nevertheless it serves to illustrate my point: that my sister and I remember playing with my father with a mixture of awe and despair.

CUT TO:

A large living room in South Africa. Sitting in armchairs pulled up around an improvised card table are two adults and two teenagers. The mother and daughter are opposite each other, as are the father and son. They are playing bridge. The mother finishes dealing and scoops up her cards with a practiced move. The son and daughter pick up their cards and start to arrange them by suit, and to do a point count. The father is studiously filling his pipe. The mother, as dealer, opens the bidding.

MOTHER: Pass.

SON: Pass.

DAUGHTER: One heart.

FATHER *(puffing on his pipe)*: Mmm. Four spades.

SON: Oh, for heaven's sake.

MOTHER: Double!

SON: Pass.

His pipe lit, the father picks up his cards and studies them.

DAUGHTER: Pass.

FATHER: You sure? What happened to all those hearts you were boasting about?

DAUGHTER: You're vulnerable.

MOTHER: And doubled.

FATHER: Redouble.

MOTHER: Pass.

The son looks long and hard at his cards. Clearly he thinks the whole thing is hopeless, but he does have five small diamonds.

SON: Five diamonds.
DAUGHTER: Double!
FATHER: Redouble!

All pass.

It is the son's hand. The daughter—her father's daughter—makes an aggressive lead of the ten of diamonds. The father, as dummy, lays down his hand. He has five diamonds to the Ace, and eighteen points.

Oh, and a void in spades.

Sometimes we make the contract. Sometimes my father can take a 17–23 point deficit and a minority trump holding and turn it into four spades.

More often we go down.

But occasionally we win in style, and no matter how many times we go four down, each time we make game against a 17–23 point spread while vulnerable, my father looks across the table at me.

"Works every time," he says with a wink. "Never fails."

.   .   .

In crosswords, as in bridge, every detail matters. In British cryptic crosswords, the first important detail is the number or numbers given after the clue to indicate the number of letters in the solution. The numbers of letters can make all the difference. For example, a "Stiff examination (4,6)" is a "post mortem," whereas a "Stiff examination (7)"[2] is an "autopsy." The skill is in learning to read what's going on behind the numbers; in learning to interpret the many possible meanings they might have. The skill is in learning to choose the meaning that makes the most sense.

Many years after my parents taught me how to play bridge, my girlfriend tries to teach me the rules of crosswords. She has been doing them for some time. The conversation follows the pattern of all these kinds of conversations.

"What you must do," she says, "is suspend reason. This is not about reason."

"Okay."

"This is not about what words mean. This is about what words don't mean."

"O-kay."

"In every clue there is a word that means the same as the answer. This is either the first word or the last word. Okay? This word—or it might be a phrase—means the same as the answer."

"So it *is* about what words mean?"

"No."

"Uh-huh."

"The rest of the clue is the parts that make up the answer."

"Good."

"Now you try."

I am mouthing the words like a child learning to read.

I try, without success. My reason politely declines to be suspended. I have a sense that this is pointless. In the world there
are bigger things afoot. But we are not in the world; we are in
our house near the Arsenal in North London.

This was New Year's Day, 1990. Romania, I remember, was
alight.

thumbs
in the
wind

Back in 1983, my girlfriend and I began our travels. We waved goodbye to the soldier at the Zimbabwean border. At the other end, the northern end of the bridge, there was another soldier. He too asked for cigarettes.

He was not a philosopher. He got cigarettes, not money.

Zimbabwe, Botswana, Zambia, Malawi.

The countries pass in a gentle blur of meals cooked over our small stove. Our nights are spent in our tent or battling mosquitoes in government rest houses.

My girlfriend and I are reasonably happy. We have no deadlines. Sometimes we move on. Sometimes we decide not to. In any case we are hitchhiking. Where we go—and how fast—depends on what lifts we get.

For my twenty-second birthday she produces a tin of berries. She has been carrying them secretly for two months. We eat them with condensed milk, and then we swim in Lake Malawi. We are tanned and fit. For the only time in my adult life I have no regard for the passage of time. When we are not swimming we read books. When we are not reading we make love by candlelight. When we are not making love we sleep. In many ways it is a wonderful life.

The miles pass. In the backs of trucks we call "bakkies" and the front seats of Mercedes, we are moving across Africa. We have conversations that take in the world. The thrilling and the banal coexist in our travels.

In Zimbabwe I make tea beneath a great baobab. Near Bulawayo the scarlet berets of Mugabe's Fifth Brigade are everywhere in evidence. It emerges only later that they have been engaged in the brutal repression of ZAPU supporters.

In Botswana an elephant explodes.

The elephant was shot in Namibia by South African troops, but it crossed into Botswana before dying. It has been dead for some time. After a week in the sun it erupts. The intestine appears to flow across the veld like cold lava. It overflows the carcass and spreads toward us. One of the guards takes a knife and punctures it. When it is punctured the smell hits us like the noise from a blast and we vomit in unison. Even the game guards throw up.

In Botswana we share the back of a bakkie with two buffalo heads. Their blood congeals on our sandals. The smell sticks with me. The young men driving the bakkie think this is terribly funny. My girlfriend and I find it less so.

In Zambia we sleep in a great four-poster bed draped with mosquito nets. In Mombasa we attend Mass in a church designed to resemble the ark. The people come in, two by two. At the beaches to the north we drift for hours in the warm salt water.

In Malawi we wait for my girlfriend to get a new passport. She is trading up, becoming Irish. To travel through Africa at this time it is necessary to have a passport other than South African. Since my father was born in Scotland, I am already British. In my passport I have entered my place of birth as "Parktown North." Parktown North is a suburb of Johannesburg. But it could easily be part of London.

My passport says that I am British and that I was born in Parktown North. It must be true.

Within what we call the "traveling community" there is a fierce market in books. We trade them as prisoners trade cigarettes. I have a much-prized copy of Hunter S. Thompson's *Fear and Loathing in Las Vegas*. It has been a complete revelation for someone coming from South Africa, and a vindication of my belief that there was a world out there of which I knew nothing—yet. I hold on to it, waiting for the right deal to come along. Eventually, under pressure from my girlfriend, I swap it for a package consisting of Evelyn Waugh's *Scoop,* two dreadful bodice-rippers that promise "to touch our heartstrings," and three back issues of *Time* magazine. I could, I know, have got more. But then again, the stories to touch our heartstrings have gold embossed writing on the covers.

One of them is dedicated "To Simon, with love." My girlfriend uses the dedication page to light a fire over which we cook bream in a tomato-and-onion base.

On our travels *Scoop* seems the appropriate thing to read. It is a wonderful tale of late imperial folly.

In it Mrs. Stitch is doing the crossword while organizing the world.

"See if 'terracotta' fits," she instructs her butler.

"'Terracotta' is too long, madam," he says in due course, "and there is no R."

To which she memorably replies "Try 'Hottentot.' It's that kind of word."

Our travels are full of that kind of word.

At Nairobi bus station we find a bus that takes us to the suburb where my mother's godmother lives. She is old, but sprightly, and she shares a colonial house in the suburbs with two other elderly women. One of them was the first white woman to climb Mount Kenya. Now they pass their twilight years sipping gin and talking faintly about the past.

In the evenings they sit and do the *Telegraph* crossword. A faithful retainer fills in the answers. He answers to the name Ben.

The elderly women try out answers and Ben corrects them with what appears to be infinite patience. The conversations go like this.

CUT TO:

A chintz room. On the walls are oil paintings of imposing relatives and fading brown maps. Above the mantelpiece there is an old rifle, together with a mounted wildebeest trophy. An old but handsome black man holds a copy of the Telegraph *in one hand and a pen in the other.*

BEN: Six letters, madam. "Country with its capital in Czechoslovakia." Six letters.

MOTHER'S GODMOTHER: Well, it's a country.

MOTHER'S GODMOTHER'S FRIEND: How many letters did you say?

BEN: Six, madam.

MGF: Six?

MG: What does it start with?

BEN: We don't know madam. It ends with Y.

MG: Y?

BEN: Yes, madam.

MGF: Why what?

MG: No, no. It ends with Y. Six letters, ending with Y.

Silence settles on the room. Ben diplomatically looks at the carpet. My girlfriend has a pen out and has written down the clue. I see from her face that she has the answer. I see from Ben's face that he has the answer. I see from the faces of the old women that there is not a glimmer of a chance that they will get the answer.

CUT TO:

MG: Its capital is in Yugoslavia?

BEN: Czechoslovakia, madam.

MG: Pity. Yugoslavia has a Y.

BEN: Yes, madam.

MGF: My John was in Czechoslovakia. In 'forty-three.

MOTHER'S GODMOTHER'S OTHER FRIEND: Czechoslovakia
    didn't exist in 'forty-three.

MGF: Didn't it? Well, then. He must have been some-
    where else.

MG: What's the capital of Czechoslovakia?

BEN: Prague, madam.

MGF (triumphantly): "Poland" has six letters!

MGOF: Does it?

MG: What about "Norway"? "Norway" ends in Y.

BEN: It is "Norway," madam.

MG: It is?

BEN: Yes, madam.

MGF: Ooh, you are good! I never get them.

MG: Next!

MGOF: Why is it Norway? Norway is nowhere near Czechoslovakia.

I do not understand the rules, and they have not been explained to me. It is a decade before I realize that Oslo, the capital of Norway is "in" CzechOSLOvakia, and that therefore
Norway "has its capital in Czechoslovakia." It is more than a
decade until I find that this clue, or variations of this clue, crop
up in much of the literature of crosswords. It is a classic of the
embedded-clue structure. Many years later I play a game with
my daughter. We agree that it is possible to exist in Liberia (2),
to get married in Sweden (3), and, best of all, to take a leak
upon the Mississippi (4).

"But that would only work," she says, "in a down clue."

Thirty years before I did, my eight-year-old daughter has
got it.

We scour a map, looking for more.

There are bent old women in Micronesia (6).

In Nairobi in 1984, Ben's face is an ebony carving. His long features betray no emotion, but there is something about his eyes
that suggests understanding and depth.

He tells me he loves English.

He tells me he loves the way we can play with our words, the
way they can mean anything.

When it is time for bed, he is dismissed. The crossword is half done.

"*Kwaheri*," the little old ladies sing out in unison.

"Good night." Ben bows, and walks backward out the room. In the morning I notice the paper on the kitchen table. I also notice that the crossword is complete.

I suspect there is more to Ben than meets the eye.

It is easy to make fun of the little old ladies in the twilight of their colonial experience. But I realize that it is not necessary for them to be good at crosswords for them to enjoy them. Being good is not the point. The point is the ritual. The point is to belong.

The crossword lets people in the suburbs of Nairobi feel they belong to the community of *Telegraph* readers. More than any other part of the paper, the experience of doing the crossword binds them in.

It reminds them who they are, and who they were.

It lets them talk about John, who may or may not have been in Czechoslovakia in 'forty-three.

By May 1984, my girlfriend and I are in Europe. I have only short trousers, and our money is running low. We have no warm clothes and have long since swapped our down sleeping bags for a large sack of Java print cotton.

I cannot believe how cold it is.

In Athens we shoplift some woolen jumpers and hurry on. Near Split in Yugoslavia we camp on a beach in the snow. In a desperate attempt to stay warm I eat more *cepavcici*, a kind of Yugoslav toad-in-the-hole, than is wise. We take refuge in a hotel in Sarajevo, where we watch the Eurovision Song Contest. It is coming "live from Luxembourg." Belle and the Devotions are doing their thing for Britain, but the contest is won by a Swedish group singing something called "Diggi-loo Diggi-ley." It is hard to take seriously. It is some years before I realize that we are not supposed to take it seriously.

It was a cold spring that year. Even in our stolen clothes we are cold. We take a bus to the outskirts of Zagreb. Years later I see a clue for Zagreb in the *Independent*. It is reasonably simple: "Sculpture of zebra around front of garden city (6)."* By the time I see this clue I have become sufficiently proficient at crosswords that I know instantly that "sculpture" is an anagram indicator. Solving it is the work of a moment.

This may be a form of progress.

North of Split, a Catholic priest teaches me pidgin Italian, in case we go that way.

"Venice," he says, "now there is a city.

"Repeat after me," he says: " '*Ho scappato da Sudafrica perché ho refutato fare la guerra.*' " I left South Africa because I refused to fight.

---

*By Phi, January 17, 2002. Anagram of "zebra" together with the G from "garden."

It is my one claim. I mouth the words without conviction.

"Where do you live?" he asks.

"In London."

This is another claim.

I wonder what London looks like.

As luck would have it, our next lift is going north through Austria rather than west, and we bypass Italy altogether. Austria and Germany pass in a green blur. Then France. And from Calais we take the ferry to Dover. It has taken six months.

In London we are spectacularly gauche.

All our way through Africa we never carried a map. Maps proved themselves highly unreliable. Instead we would ask directions and, despite inaccurate distances and confused place names, we never got lost.

This doesn't work in London.

In London everything is mapped.

From Dover we get a lift that drops us in Catford, a nondescript suburb of southeast London. It is a Sunday morning, and raining. I have no idea where Catford is. By the time we get there it feels as though we have been in traffic and between terraced houses forever. All the billboards say SCARGILL. This is the time of the miners' strike, and Arthur Scargill is president of the National Union of Mineworkers. But I do not know who he is.

I look around. So this is what London looks like. London

looks like a gray dream painted on wet brown bricks, and littered with chocolate wrappers.

At Catford there is a sign that says CENTRAL LONDON. We plonk our rucksacks in the rain, and stick out our thumbs.

Now it seems incredible. It seems incredible that we could have tried to hitchhike from Catford to "London." But we did.

In fact we are not heading for "Central London" at all. We are heading for Ealing, where my girlfriend has an aunt. After several hours a car stops. We are not surprised by the delay. In Africa we would often wait five or six hours for a lift. Once, at Francistown in Botswana, we waited two days.

In London the driver who picks us up keeps a straight face. He takes us to Hammersmith, which he assures us is near Ealing.

It is, near enough. In Africa we could have walked it. Here we feel conspicuous, even stupid. We take the tube for the last stage of our journey.

In Ealing it is still raining. I am not troubled, for I have a waterproof poncho.

But nor do I feel I have come home.

Then again, I am not quite the corpse we met on the bridge over the brown Limpopo River.

I have certain resources.

I have an image of myself.

I have a story to tell.

4

arrivals

London presents itself as a buffet of competing stories. You can help yourself. Eat as much as you like. The trouble is that everybody has one, and they clamor to be heard. I find I cannot interpret them all. I cannot tell the good ones from the bad.

This is the summer of 1984.

I find also that while I may have a story, I lack an audience. My girlfriend has heard it before, and the people at the pizza place where I have found work do not seem to be interested. The pizza place is one of a large chain, and I am in charge of making the dough. In a matter of weeks I have qualified as a "dough master," and I have a certificate to prove it. My fellow dough master has a Ph.D. from Moscow University and a supplementary qualification from somewhere in Poland. He comes, he says, from Volgograd, and he spends long evenings over the kneading machine telling me of his dreams of freedom. I find it amiable enough to listen to his dreams of freedom. He keeps a dictionary on the shelf above the kneading machine and is apt to choose words at random, and to ask what they mean. "Ineffable," he says. "Now, what is this?" Mostly I am able to help, though in this case I find it hard to capture the essence of the word. Much later I find that it has been turned into a glorious crossword clue: "Impossible to express in a four-letter word? (9)."[3] I was reminded of this when someone told me this clue: "Flattery is no effin' use (7)."*

Otherwise there is not much to entertain us. Occasionally a punter in the restaurant does a runner without paying the bill, and we "backroom boys" get to chase him down the High Street. We enjoy these moments of release. We laugh and shout insults. I wonder what would happen if we actually caught someone.

"Lucky bastard," says Jacko, who does the dishes. "I nearly had him then." Jacko was born to Dutch parents in Mysore and dreams of being a knife thrower in a circus. He always has a knife with him. He tests the blade against his scarred thumb.

My friend from Volgograd and I are unhappy. The hours in the pizza place are long and the pay is low. We decide to organize. We will form a union. We will go on strike. We hold meetings after hours. We have nothing to lose, we tell our fellow pizza workers, but our chains.

At this stage in our lives we are not big on irony.

---

*INEFFABLE and UNCTION, meaning "flattery," where there is no F in "function" = use.

We write letters to management and request face-to-face meetings. We write to the Transport and General Workers' Union. They send an organizer to talk to us.

"We haven't had much luck in the fast-food sector," he says. "You all move around too much. Too many of you are from abroad."

We apologize for being from abroad.

Virtually everyone in the pizza place is from abroad. Management consists of two men, Ali, who comes from northern Cyprus, and Dan, who comes from County Cork in Ireland. Ali and Dan ignore our letters of protest at our working conditions, and so we post them to Head Office. Head Office, in obvious panic, sends two men in suits to talk to us. They explain that the company does not recognize any union. They say that there are well-established procedures for dealing with grievances. They point out the way the country is going. Unions are, apparently, a thing of the past. Look at how the miners are being torn apart. The way forward is for staff and management to work together. If we have grievances, of course, we are free to talk about them.

When we talk about our grievances they explain that higher wages mean fewer jobs. Then they threaten us with the sack, and dock our pay for the time we are in the meeting with them. Afterward my friend tells me there are no unemployed people in the Soviet Union.

"But they all hate their jobs," he says.

I find I miss South Africa. At least there I knew what game we were playing.

For £90 I buy a motorcycle. On downhill slopes it goes faster than I can walk.

My girlfriend and I ride around London. We ride from Ealing to Hyde Park, and Regent's Park. We discover that the easy regularity of the map of the London Tube bears no resemblance to the real London above ground. The Tube map suggests that the trains go in straight lines, and that the stops are evenly spaced. The truth is that London's layout suggests a city planned by a horse following a carrot wobbling on a string. Roads twist and turn. Distances expand and contract, depending on how much traffic there is. For us it becomes a game to navigate. We delight in getting lost. We ride the wrong direction down one-way streets. But gradually we find our bearings. We visit Kew Gardens and Richmond Park. We cruise up the Mall and chug along the Embankment. One day I ride to Lords to watch the cricket. Clive Lloyd is leading the West Indies to victory over England. I sit in the sun and watch the rout.

Around me, also basking in the hot weather, people do the crossword.

Some of them do three or four in the course of the day. They call out clues to each other.

I remember the three old ladies in Nairobi.

One of the few English batsman to make any runs is Allan Lamb, who is not from England, but is from Cape Town. More specifically he is from Greenpoint, which is where I lived with my girlfriend before we stuck out the thumbs that carried us all the way to London. I am not fooled by the program notes, which say Allan Lamb is from Northampton.

On the strength of my "experience" as a teacher, I get a job in a youth club in south London. The club is patronized almost exclusively by black people. It has a large sports hall, a snooker room, and a coffee bar, and is set in a hilltop of council estates in Wandsworth. Although our work is supposedly with these "youth," many of whom are older than I, we in fact spend much of our time working on "policies." We have policies for almost everything. We are anti-racist and anti-sexist. We positively discriminate in favor of young women. We favor "participatory democracy." For those things not covered by our policies, we have minutes. We hold daylong and weeklong meetings, and minute them passionately.

When we are not having meetings, I play pool with the youths. For this I am paid £4.80 an hour.

One afternoon there is a conflict on the estate between black and white youths. According to evidence given in court, some white youths have pushed a black child off a first-floor balcony. Some black youths have responded by severely beating one of the whites with a cricket bat. Within moments there are many police cars around, and a helicopter overhead. This is a time of heightened racial tension in Britain. Charges of what the newspapers call "the new offense of affray" are laid against the black youths. I am puzzled that no one lays charges against the white youths. "This is England," says my colleague. "You don't understand."

I am a character witness in the ensuing court case. I say that I know one of the black youths charged to be a person of fine and upstanding character. I say that I am confident he will hold on to the job that he, on the advice of his lawyer, has taken for the duration of the case.

In the hallway outside the courtroom, the solicitor for another of the accused is doing the crossword. He was born in Barbados, and came to live in London when he was eight. I ask him when he learned to do the crossword, and he laughs. "It's part of your legal training here," he says.

It was only many years later that I realized he was joking. At about the same time I discovered that crosswords top the Home Office guidelines for approved entertainment for prison inmates. Prison governors are encouraged to make crosswords available in prisons. They are a form of "peaceful recreation." They keep prisoners "in touch," and they keep their minds "active." Many years later, a correspondent to the *Times* confirmed this. His father had suffered from acute Alzheimer's, but throughout almost his entire illness he was able to do the *Times* crossword.

Back in 1984, the young man is acquitted. Justice, apparently, has been seen to be done.

At the youth club we play more pool and kick a football around. It is not immediately clear how this discriminates in favor of young women.

Later two of the youths from the club achieve of degree of

notoriety as the "Serpentine Pirates." They have struck on the novel idea of mugging people while they row their boats about the lake in the center of Hyde Park. They threaten to tip tourists into the water unless they hand over money and jewelry. It works so well the first time that they try again. And again. But they haven't thought this through. Those who have been mugged return to shore and call the police.

When the youths step ashore the police arrest them. No amount of character endorsement is going to get them off.

There comes a point when I can no longer take seriously my "work" in the youth club, nor our ongoing and increasingly primitive accumulation of minutes. I resign and scan the newspapers, desperate for a job and for news from home. I spend some time in Italy, where I learn Italian by reading the newspapers.

There is plenty of news from home. CINQUE NERI UCCISI is a popular headline.

The townships have erupted. Every day seems to bring fresh news that more "blacks have been killed." Troops have moved into Katlehong and Mamelodi. Archbishop Tutu has won the Nobel Peace Prize. It is far more interesting than the distorted and diffuse race and class politics of south London.

I begin to think of myself as an exile.

I am very depressed.

departures

Perhaps eighteen months after I arrived in London, I became restless and started to travel again. I returned to London each time, but I had only to touch down at Heathrow to start thinking about where and when I might move again. This state of mind lasted several years.

In Zimbabwe I meet up with my parents. We swim in the clean green waters of the eastern Highlands. We send straw boats crashing off the Mtarazi Falls. Hundreds of feet below, they land in Mozambique. I envy them their journey though not, quite, their arrival.

I make speaking tours in Europe and the United States. I am

a conscientious objector, but not a pacifist. For the left at this time this is a helpful distinction.

In Germany I make the same speech forty times in two weeks. The audiences clap politely and ask me questions I am wholly unqualified to answer. They want to know, for example, "what it is like in the townships." I have no idea what it is like in the townships, other than what I read in the papers. I tell a story about the time I was a teacher and crashed my motorbike with one of my pupils riding on the back. We skidded on the wet road and slid across the tarmac. Fortunately neither of us was seriously hurt, but the girl and I ended up on the road, our left legs pinned to the ground by the weight of the machine.

This was in Mitchell's Plain, a "coloured" area, but hardly a "township."

A coloured man approached and I smiled gratefully for the help he was about to give us.

Instead he addressed the girl.

"*Ja,*" he said. "*Jy sien wat gebeur as jy met 'n whitey ry?*" You see what happens when you ride with a white man? He went off cackling while I strained to lift the bike off our legs.

Years later I told this story to a prominent member of the new black elite. We were at a diplomatic reception in Pretoria in a smart hotel across the road from the Union Buildings.

"He was right," the prominent member of the new elite said, which I felt rather missed the point. He scooped some caviar onto a piece of black bread.

. . .

In Germany in 1987, I am on stronger ground talking about the role of the military in propping up the apartheid state, and the importance of conscientious objection. There is much talk of *Schwarze-gegen-Schwarze Gewalt*. Black-on-black violence has become a refrain of those friendly to the apartheid government. I am able easily to rebut this argument. In any case I am preaching to the converted.

The converted include a man from Bremerhaven who has achieved a degree of notoriety by pelting the German Chancellor, Helmut Kohl, with a cabbage. The visual pun—*kohl* is German for "cabbage"—appealed to certain sections of the popular press.

He and I become friendly. He asks when I will go home and, against the party line, I tell him I doubt I ever will. "It never really felt like home," I say.

"Does England?"

"No."

"But where, then?" he asks. "You must belong somewhere."

Must I?

I try the United States, where I watch fireworks over the Charles River on the Fourth of July. I listen to the nasal drip of

Oliver North's testimony in the Iran-Contra hearings. At Walden Pond I swim in the spring-fed lake. Henry David Thoreau claimed to be able to tell the season there to within two days by looking at the plants around his cabin.

I was struggling to remember the year.

I try London again. I start to read the newspapers, and now, instead of turning straight to the "International News," I am interested in the sports pages and the leader columns. Stories have greater resonance. I can connect events that happened this year with events that happened the year before. I am no longer a blank sheet. It is as though a grid has been drawn, and even some clues have been written. But I do not yet know how to fill it in.

I become a regular reader of the *Guardian*. For the first time since I arrived, I start reading books. I discover Dickens, and Jack London's *People of the Abyss*. I discover Orwell and Jonathan Raban. I read and reread *Homage to Catalonia* and *Old Glory*. Two friends and I walk from Barcelona to the Pyrenees and back again. We eat olives and spit the pips. On Orwell's advice we avoid the *chorizo*.

One friend is South African; the other is Irish. We spend our time covering huge distances and debating the riddle that England poses. All countries are a puzzle, we decide. My Irish friend has been reading a book about Charles Dodgson, better known as Lewis Carroll, who was an enthusiast—some say the inventor—of doublets. In doublets the idea is simple. You take two words of equal length, and try to get from one to the other by interposing a number of other words. Each other word differs from the previous one by only one letter. You can, for example, get from "east" to "west" by interposing "last" and "lest." A well-known example devised by an American named Sam Loyd is to get from "ape" to "man" in the fewest possible number of steps.

My friends and I play this game as we cover the miles. We turn "talking" into "singing" and "slow" into "fast." We cannot, for the life of us, turn "foreign" into "English."

We talk about identity, about who we want to be. Some years later my Irish friend takes me to lunch in a newly fashionable restaurant in Clerkenwell. He has let his hair grow long and is wearing a sweater that hangs almost to his knees. He has made a decision, he says, to be a woman.

Perhaps anything really is possible.

I must belong somewhere.

I try Italy, where a comrade from the young Communists takes me around Rome on her Vespa. The days are hot and the nights are warm. I make speeches of solidarity with Romanies and Ethiopians.

I am talking through my hat.

One night we go to see Bruce Springsteen play the Olympic Stadium. His mother is of Italian extraction, and he has a huge local following there.

"*Stanco?*" he roars to the crowd. "Are you tired?"

"*No!*"

"*Stanco?*"

"*No!*"

The crowd holds up lighters on a windless night.

I realize that I am very, very tired.

But I misdiagnose my fatigue, and throw myself further into being South African. I have a job with a South African television news agency and the material I sell is being seen all over the world. We are starting to produce longer pieces, documentaries. We are making money. I take over a newspaper business, selling South Africa's alternative press to exiles in London and elsewhere. I start and manage a housing cooperative for exiles.

From time to time I meet with senior exiles to give an account of myself. I give myself glowing reports and look enthusiastic. But my heart is not in it. It cannot possibly last.

I think back on the story I have to tell and realize that it does not answer the question I am most frequently asked: "So when do you think you will go back home?" I tend to shrug when asked this question. I do not say what I am thinking.

I will go home when I have one.

cracks
in the
wall

It is New Year's Day, 1990. My girlfriend and I have taken the first steps toward creating a home by buying part of a house near the Arsenal Football Club in north London. In our house, my girlfriend is making another attempt to teach me the basics of crosswords. She has recently spent some time in New York City. She calls it, therefore, "Crosswords 101," in the manner of East Coast colleges.

"Take 'pretty girl in crimson rose,'" she says. "Eight letters. What does it mean?"

This is a dangerous question to ask me. At this point in my life I am inclined to see meanings where there are none. I am inclined to give a very personal interpretation of things. I bring to them meanings that do not exist. I project anxieties onto the most innocent of words. Perhaps it is because I have been involved in telling and selling stories about South Africa. I have become accustomed to the pattern of these stories, to their structure. They start, invariably, with some cold assessment of the evils of the apartheid government. They move swiftly to the resolute defiance of the people who will topple the government. They end, invariably, with a statement that the collapse of apartheid is only a matter of time. But even at Christmas 1989, you would have been hard pressed to find a pundit to measure that time in years rather than decades.

I have, therefore, lots of anxieties to project. I am still inclined to focus on containment. I do not have the kind of confidence that says stories should be allowed to breathe.

My girlfriend knows this, and she does not let me answer her question.

"It means that we have a pretty girl, and she is wearing something red, or pink," she says. "She is wearing something that suits her prettiness. Prettiness, girls, roses—they all go together."

I nod. "Got it," I say.

"It means," says my girlfriend, "nothing of the sort."

I nod again. I am keeping up.

I smile encouragingly.

"That," says my girlfriend, "is what they want you to think it means. What it actually means is either the first word or the last word. What it actually means is 'rose.'"

"It does?"

"It does."

"Okay."

Outside in the street, Arsenal fans are shuffling by after a game. It is already dark but I can tell from the suppressed hum of satisfaction that Arsenal has won.[4] There is a climbing rose in our front garden. I am vaguely aware that it is not a genuine climbing rose. It is an ordinary rose that has been allowed to climb. Parts of it hang down and drag on the ground. Its red petals look purple in the orange light.

I remember thinking that nothing was ever as it seemed. I remember wondering whether I would ever deconstruct the face England presents to the world.

CUT TO:

A sparely furnished living room in north London. A man and a woman are seated on a crimson sofa. She is doing the cross-word. He is half paying attention to her. In the corner of the room a television is carrying silent news images from the year.

WOMAN: Here's one you can do.

MAN: Thank you.

WOMAN: So give me another word for "crimson."

MAN: Crimson?

WOMAN: Another word for "crimson."

MAN: Red?

WOMAN: Very good.

The woman writes R E _ _ _ _ _ D on a piece of paper. She looks at the man expectantly.

WOMAN: And "pretty girl"?

MAN: You?

The woman looks at him with affectionate contempt.

WOMAN: I'm not a girl.

There is a moment when they do not speak. Outside the window a football crowd thins.

WOMAN *(losing patience)*: Belle. "Belle" is another word for "pretty girl." And then we put "belle" which means "pretty girl" inside "red" which means "crimson," and we get R-E-B-E-L-L-E-D, "rebelled." *Et voilà.*

MAN: "Rebelled" means "rose"?

WOMAN: It does.

MAN: Hmmm. *(He pauses.)* How?

On the television screen there is a story about Romania. The people of Romania are rebelling. We see again how they rush Ceauşescu's palace. He was shot unceremoniously on Christmas Day. Wearing black leather coats they walk past his slumped body. Nobody wears crimson.

"As in Prague in 'sixty-eight," says my girlfriend. "As in rose up and overthrew the regime. Rose up as in Soweto and Paris and Leipzig. You remember. You were there."

I am feigning stupidity.

But really I have got it.

I was there.

Not in Soweto, you understand. I was not in Soweto until later. But I was in Leipzig.

Somewhere between arriving in England in 1984 and doing Crosswords 101 with my girlfriend in 1990, I had become established as a television producer. Near the end of 1989, I was in Leipzig, in what was then the German Democratic Republic, for the film festival. I was there when the crowds were gathering. And I had various kinds of status.

I am, first, a guest of the government, since I represent some films that are to be shown in the festival. Second, I am a journalist and have a press card, which means I have a form of access and of legitimacy. And I have an easy manner and a broad smile. I find that I am able to move smoothly between different worlds. One world has a host of minor officials of the German Democratic Republic. They are sipping wine and eating from great platters of cold meat and pickles. Another world is a bohemian mix of filmmakers and their acolytes. We sit in underground bars and debate the world.

And there is another world that appears to me to be passing us by. In this world, the people of Leipzig are silently and calmly bringing down their government. There is no sign of it in the great ballroom in the building on Sachsenplatz, but within days the entire edifice of the East German state will have crumbled.

By the time I was in Leipzig there were daily demonstrations in the city's great square. Toward dusk the people would begin to gather outside the churches of St. Nicholas and St. Thomas. But their numbers were too great. The overspill filled other squares. By early November, the demonstrators would number two or three hundred thousand people. Half a million even. A public-address system would be erected, and pamphlets passed around. Speaker after speaker would harangue the crowd, while the crowd looked silently back. Not for the first time in my life, I had a sense that the crowd was way ahead of the rhetoric. The crowd seemed to know that change was imminent. The orators on the podium appeared only to think that change was possible.

I remember standing on the balcony above the square and watching the silent crowd, and wondering at the orderliness of their gathering. Only in retrospect was it possible to call it a revolution. At the time it was a small protest, a suggestion that the past forty years were an affront to the dignity of the people, no more.

After a while I tire of watching the silent, strong crowd in Leipzig and go inside to share the tables decked with food for minor officials and guests of the government. I am, after all, such a guest.

But I am struggling to read the signs.

I am struggling to understand the rules.

Like a crossword clue, history never quite makes sense at first reading. The surface is plausible, but discordant. We need a second reading to impose order.

. . .

I traveled to Leipzig by train from Berlin. The train is filled with people whose stories I cannot imagine. A Vietnamese man is carrying a huge bunch of bananas. Recently there have been stories of attacks on Vietnamese *Gastarbeiter*.

Only they don't call them that.

Under socialism, all workers are one.

Even when they beat them up and steal their bananas, or when they stand silently in a square in Leipzig, cupping candles against a still wind.

Two days later I am back in Berlin, at Checkpoint Charlie, which is the crossing point between east and west. The film festival is over and the revolution is just beginning. Hungary has opened its borders. There is a sense all over Europe that millions of people are on the move.

To my surprise I find that at Checkpoint Charlie the East German authorities will not let me leave because I have a fistful of ostmarks. I have a fistful of ostmarks because the film festival has paid me per diems.

I neither drink nor smoke, and there is precious little else worth buying.

I have therefore been unable to find any way in which to spend my per diems. I buy meals for strangers, and still I have a pile of per diems. When asked by the border guards whether I had any ostmarks I pulled from my pocket a wad of cash.

I offer them to the border guards.

"Take them," I say, "you have them. Really. *Bitte*."

They arrest me for attempted bribery. They hold me against a wall and speak through tight lips. The peaks of their army caps match the pressed dark fury of their lips.

But I have official papers.

I have been a guest of the government. I have eaten their cold meats, while outside in the square the people waited for history to catch up. The guards decide to take a different approach.

In reading a crossword clue it is sometimes necessary to take a different approach. I recently, for example, spent long hours looking at "Hormone red in Lana Turner (9)."[5] I even went so far as to look up some of the things that Lana Turner is purported to have said during her lifetime. Lana Turner is purported to have said, "A successful man is one who makes more money than a wife can spend. A successful woman is one who can find such a man."

"Yeah, right," snorted my girlfriend, who was with me at the time. My girlfriend is not a fan of the philosophical musings of Hollywood stars from the forties and fifties. She thinks they lack the gravitas that comes with having been part of the women's movement in the late seventies.

Looking up the sayings of Lana Turner, while amusing in its own way, did little to advance my understanding of the clue. It was only when I took another approach that I got it. The other approach I took was to think of "Turner" as the anagram indicator, not as the name of a star of the forties and fifties.

And the anagram was of "red in Lana," and the answer was that well-known synthetic hormone, Adrenalin. Soon after this, another *Guardian* crossword setter told me it was not the first time "Turner," as opposed to "turner," had been used as an anagram indicator. The approach was different for me, but not for those who had been there before.

At this time anagrams seem to me to be the poor cousins of the crossword world, although in fact they need not be. I am beginning to realize that the art of the anagram is not the process of finding the "other words," but the process of telling the story that encapsulates the words. "Girlfriend," for example, is an anagram of "direr fling," and of "fling rider," and of "rifling red," and of a whole host of other seemingly unconnected words. The art of the setter is to take those unconnected words and to bind them with his wit.

Anagrams—*ars magna,* as the old joke goes—have a checkered history. In one sense they are the most obvious clues, and editors sometimes have to limit the number of anagrams used in a single puzzle. If the average puzzle in a 15 x 15 grid has thirty-six words, then, as a rule of thumb, there should be no more than six anagrams in the puzzle. This gets slightly confusing when there are partial anagrams in every clue. Part of the skill for the setter is to find ways of using unlikely indicators to show that it is an anagram, and then to find words that work "naturally" as the anagram itself. One of the *Guardian* setters calls himself Bunthorne. In a recent puzzle[6] he used the following as anagram indicators: "Contentious," "Fillets," "Failed," "Mess," "Other," and "Foreign."

It is possible to find a similar list in almost all puzzles that occur in broadsheet papers these days. In another we find a less exotic list: "absurd," "organized," "trained," and "somehow."[7] From time to time we find truly original indicators. I took particular pleasure in "The Nora Batty is someone else (7)."[8] Nora Batty is a much-loved character in a long-running BBC comedy called *Last of the Summer Wine*. But this clue—as always—has nothing to do with the surface meaning. In this one, as with Lana Turner, the surname is used as an anagram indicator, and the answer is "another."

At Checkpoint Charlie toward the end of 1989 a border guard accompanies me back into East Berlin. I regret that I never learned his name. He marches me to a bank. He watches me while I open a bank account. The man at the counter gives me a little book. It says I have four hundred and thirty ostmarks and that these are as good as any marks anywhere.

In particular, my little book says that these marks are as good as deutschmarks.

We all tell ourselves stories.

Once I have a bank account and have failed completely to subvert the state by exporting ostmarks or bribing border guards, I am allowed to leave East Berlin.

By this time it is dark, and there is a light mist as I walk through Checkpoint Charlie to the other side. I have no idea that within weeks this place will be history. The cobblestones on the bridge seem unnaturally big, because of the slanting light. The slanting neon light that makes the cobbles seem big is all coming from the west.

On the western side of the Wall I stand with others as they chip away at it. I know my girlfriend will be cross if I do not bring home a piece. I find myself reluctant though to swing at it with the abandon of those around me. I know from my own experiences that periods of violent transition have their price. I remember thinking it would be better to show more caution. But still, I took my piece of the Wall and flew back to London.

A few weeks later I did Crosswords 101 with my girlfriend.

At the time it didn't seem important.

They were just words on a page.

Soon after that the rumors come true. The South African government announces that the African National Congress, the Communist Party, and other political organizations are no longer banned. Mandela is shortly to be released. Exiles will be welcomed home. Things will change.

On February 2, 1990, our house at the Arsenal erupts into a spontaneous party. The upstairs floor throbs with music. People get spectacularly drunk. Toward dawn the survivors gather in our living room. There are conversations about where people will go to live. Some will go back to their hometowns. Others plan to move to Johannesburg or Pretoria, to be "where the action is."

An old friend asks me where I will go.

"You must be kidding," I say. "I'm just glad it's over."

Before the words are out I realize that for him, and for most of the people at our house that night, things are only beginning. Things are beginning for me too, but differently.

Within weeks my girlfriend is pregnant.

rumors
of
rain

My third lesson in crosswords, like my first, takes place in Africa. In Chad in the summer of 1991.

I have taken a job at a British television company, and I am in Chad to make a film about the work of a British NGO, which is doing various things to make life less hard for the people of Chad.

The person who teaches me about crosswords works for the NGO. She has a copy of the *Guardian* and is looking at its crossword. She starts telling me the differences between the various papers. I know where they stand politically, but my friend seems to think that it is the crossword, more than anything, that defines the character of the newspaper. This is a new idea to me, and I ask her to explain.

"The *Guardian* crossword is not," she tells me, "like the

Telegraph. This is not only a matter of taste. It's a question of style, and of personality. It's a matter of attitude, and of how you understand the world." Many years later an eminent managing editor of the *Times* told me the old newspaper maxim: "They come for the news, they stay for the features." And in particular they stay for the obituaries and the crossword.

I am not yet ready to form allegiances on the basis of obituaries, but I am interested to know more about crosswords. I have an inkling that there might be something in this.

My friend says something else.

She says, "It makes such a difference if you know who the setter is. If you know who the setter is, you're halfway there."

The setter in this case is Rufus. Sitting in Chad it does not seem possible to me to know someone called Rufus, but my teacher seems to think she does know him.

"He's one of the easiest," she says. "That's why I like him.

"That's not his real name," she adds.

We are in a town called Oum Hadjer, which is halfway to the Sudan. This depends, of course, on where you are coming from, but our journey has started in the capital, N'djamena. Oum Hadjer is halfway from N'djamena to the Sudan.

Oum Hadjer is a barracks town situated on the Batha River. Perhaps 15,000 people live there, in neat compounds with guttering that sticks out from the mud walls as if to test the weather. The squares are swept clean, and women hang brightly colored cloth to dry on the trees by the river. Halfway across the river a military truck has become stuck. There is a great commotion as preparations are made to tow it out. I have read somewhere that Chad at this time has less than 300 miles of tarred road. It is not hard to believe, for none reach Oum Hadjer. But at the sole crossing point there is a concrete weir, and the truck has lost its footing. Small children on pirogues pole out to the center of the stream and attach a cable to the truck. They control the pirogues with a facility born of many generations.

Once the cable is attached, the children move away. The driver, who has been sitting on the roof, climbs inside. The cable is attached to another truck on the southern bank, and we watch as the cable takes the strain. Nothing moves. Onshore a small group of people start to push the tow truck. They push harder and harder. Wheels grind against sand. Suddenly the truck on shore starts forward. We all look back to see that the vehicle in the middle of the river has not moved. Its bumper has been ripped off, though, and is now creating a wake fifty meters downstream.

"The trouble," says a man near me, "is we have had rains."

Which, given that we are on the arid fringe of the world's largest desert, is one way of looking at it.

The Batha River, which flows through the middle of Oum Hadjer, intrigues me. It runs east to west and west to east. Sometimes simultaneously.

The direction in which the Batha flows depends entirely on where there have been rains. If there have been rains in the east, the river flows west. If there have been rains in the west, the river flows east. If there has been rain in both the east and the west, the two ends of the river can flow toward the middle. If there has been rain in the middle, the river can flow east and west.

In this respect the Batha River seems to me to be like a crossword clue. A crossword clue can start at either end. It depends entirely on where the rains have been in the imagination of the setter. A crossword clue can flow in upon itself and can come from nowhere. There are many examples of crossword clues that flow without there having been rain at all. Take for example this clue: "Play Ankoolger (4,4,2,5)." This appeared in a puzzle that had as a theme the names of dramatic works of the twentieth century. Other answers were *Waiting for Godot* and *The Iceman Cometh*. At the time this clue appeared, my girlfriend and I were sitting together on the sofa, with perhaps half an eye apiece on the television. From a close textual reading of what followed you will see how our roles have changed.

CUT TO:

A living room in north London. The room is larger than before, although it conforms to the standard layout for Victorian terraced housing. There are some works of art on the walls, and bookshelves filled with books. There are various artifacts from different parts of Africa . . .

MAN: Here's a good one. "Play Ankoolger." Four, four, two, five.[9]

WOMAN: Let me see that.

The man hands the woman the paper. The woman looks at it, and then at the man.

WOMAN: Oh, I don't know. What the hell is Ankoolger? Is it some bloody computer game or something?

Pause.

WOMAN (*cont.*): Who set this anyway? *Paul?* Oh, well then.

Pause.

WOMAN (*cont.*): Anyway, what are you looking so smug about? I can remember when watching you do the crossword was like watching a goldfish think. So don't give me that.

Pause.

WOMAN (*cont.*): Oh, all right. What is it?

MAN: It's quite a good clue, actually. Works really rather nicely.

At this point the woman throws the paper at the man and starts to walk out.

WOMAN (*parting shot*): Perhaps we should get two papers delivered.

MAN: Ah, don't look at me like that, sweetie.

WOMAN: Like what?

MAN: You know. Look back in anger.

WOMAN: What are you . . . (*Then she gets it.*) Oh for heaven's sake! The bastard. You bastard! (*Pause.*) That's so good.

It is a lovely clue. The same setter told me once that the secret to setting crosswords is to take ordinary words and to make them extraordinary. He meant little by this. For him it was just a statement of the obvious. But to me it captured the essence of the artistic endeavor that lies beneath the everyday puzzles. All are filled with ordinary words. Great clues render the words memorable and the clues unforgettable.

In Chad in 1991 it is possible to think of the landscape as both ordinary and remarkable. Mostly there is no rain at all, and the River Batha shows no sign of flowing anywhere. At this stage in my knowledge of crosswords this describes how crosswords are. I look at them blankly. Neither I nor the clue show any sign of moving.

One evening I swim in the Batha. It is like swimming in mud.

I need not tell you that this too is how I experience doing the crossword at this stage in my life.

It is not immediately clear what the point is.

I am uncertain of which way to go.

I cannot see my feet.

And yet I emerge strangely relaxed.

Emerging from the Batha at dusk on a hot, hot day, I towel myself off with the *kikoi* cloth I bought in Mombasa when my girlfriend and I were traveling to London.

Evening has settled on the town. There is the scent of wood fires. As the sun sets it briefly appears that the entire western edge of the Sahel is on fire. It is only many years later that I

wonder whether "on fire" would be a legitimate anagram indicator, because I have spotted that "Sahel" lends itself to anagrams. Leash. Shale. Heals.

Oum Hadjer, at the time in question, is under the control of
a *sous-Prefet*. It is not long after what the Chadians refer to as
les evenements. "The events" means an earlier coup attempt that
failed.

At the time we are there the bullet marks are fresh on the mud
walls, and the soldiers ride around in the backs of Toyota pickup
trucks and wave their Kalashnikovs in the air. And yet the people
of Oum Hadjer appear to go about their business with a will. On
the riverbank, kids play in silhouette against the setting sun.

Later in the evening on which I swam in the Batha the television crew and I are guests of one of the families of Oum
Hadjer. Earlier in the day the *sous-Prefet* has given us a goat,
which is to be slaughtered for the evening's festivities.

We are all seated on a large mat. There are perhaps thirty
people. Food is passed around. To go with the goat there is
chicken, and spices and dates. There is sorghum too, and millet,
and small pastries made from wheat. We dip sorghum balls in
goat gravy and scoop up handfuls of diced-and-spiced chicken.
There are none of the French goodies we bought in N'djamena.
There are no croissants, nor baguettes, nor are there the otherwise ubiquitous tinned *petit pois*.

We eat well. I remember it still as one of the best meals I've
ever had. Hunger can do that, but so can good food and a sun-
set from heaven.

After the meal our host invites us to tell stories.

He tells a glorious story. Perhaps it is the way he tells it, or perhaps it is the fact that he speaks in Arabic, and the Arabic is translated first into French and then into English, but what comes across is a very precise and poetic tale. It reminds me more than anything of the rhythms of spirituals from the American South. Perhaps it is just that he has a voice like Billie Holiday.

The story he tells us while seated cross-legged on the ground involves a green creature that lives in the water and emerges only during the longest dry seasons. The green creature emerges from the river and stalks the land. It claims the weak and takes them. When the rains come the green beast disappears, and the weak are gone.

We listen carefully, enchanted by the food and the smells, and by a late moon rising. Despite the translation, it is not hard to make sense of it.

There's a man going round, taking names.

It is a universal story.

It is the story of all Chadians, for all time.

A year later I am in the Philippines, making a different film. More specifically I am in Mindanao, the large southern island of the archipelago, to witness a particular cultural phenomenon. This concerns a group of indigenous people on the slopes of Mount Apo whose livelihoods have slowly, inexorably, been whittled away to nothing by the insatiable demands of encroaching "low-landers." The lowlanders are themselves poor peasant farmers.

The resulting disputes have led to increasingly frequent

armed clashes between the indigenous people and the low-
landers. By and large the indigenous people lose, and they find
themselves living an increasingly marginal existence high up
the slopes of this sleeping volcano.

The response of the agencies that would help the indigenous
people is interesting. They have, for example, funded a theater
group to work with the indigenous people. The theater group
leader explains to me what they are doing.

"We're helping them tell their story," he says. "We use music
and dance, theater and mime, and through this the people remember who they are. Obviously they need to defend themselves, but you don't have anything to defend if you don't know
who you are."

I watch as a group of women dance a story of distant fires. It
is a story of their lives that goes back in time, and yet is of the
present. They sing and ululate, and all night there is a beating
of drums. To this day I cannot shake the memory of the face of
one woman whose death in the dance represented the death of
their way of life.

Miles below us, glittering in the distant foothills of Mount
Apo, it is possible to see the encircling fires of the lowlanders.

I appreciate the power of the indigenous people's story, but I
suspect that the encircling fires will win. Knowing who you are
is only the beginning.

When in Oum Hadjer our host asks me to tell a story, I find I am
at a loss. I do not know what stories Britain tells about itself.

I am the producer, and I have a crew. I feel I should tell a story that is inclusive, which is about all of "us," but I feel unequal to the task. It falls to my teacher to tell us a story, but when she does, she tells it in French.

I do not know if I am included.

Later that night I look again at Rufus. I am armed with two things. One is the knowledge that he is "the easiest." The other is that if you know the setter, you are halfway there.

I would like to be halfway there.

I do not feel I have even begun.

I wonder if it is possible to know Rufus.

I wonder where one starts.

A clue catches my eye. "Émigré beaten up by the authorities (6)." By now I know enough to recognize an anagram.

"Regime," I say to myself as I fall asleep.

This is where I date my beginning.

Later, in London, my teacher has returned from her time in Chad and is wondering where to live. I find myself arguing in favor of England.

I say it is a good place to live. I argue the merits of the liberal chattering class. I mention Radio Four and the broadsheet press. I mention Britain's tradition of internationalism and the welcome it has given me. I mention also Britain's tradition of dissent, the undercurrent of rebellion that runs through what otherwise appears to be a peaceful society.

My teacher is not convinced.

She sees no sign of dissent. This was 1992, after all, and in the General Election of that year the electorate endorsed the Conservative Party's decision to replace Margaret Thatcher with John Major. The Tories will be in government—though not, as the outgoing Chancellor Norman Lamont memorably put it, "in power"—for five more years.

I also mention crosswords. I repeat to her what she told me when we were in Chad. Crosswords tell stories about ourselves. Crosswords express our humanity. Crosswords are the representation of an unspoken bond, between setter and solver, between paper and reader, between words and life. And British crosswords do it better than any others.

"The thing about crosswords," she says, "is that they travel. You can get them anywhere."

"Yes," I say, "but they come from somewhere specific. They are not themselves, if you separate them from the culture that created them."

"Oh, I think you can," she said. "They travel, we travel. We can all take on new identities. We can become who we want to become.

"Look at you," she said.

I remember my mother's aunt in Nairobi. I remember the *Telegraph* crossword, and how it rang in that household louder than Big Ben.

I was not yet ready to look at myself too closely.

spit
and
patience

And still I did not have critical mass. I had not yet taken the fateful step that turned me from someone with a passing interest in a minor cultural form into someone with a passion for crosswords.

Not surprisingly, perhaps, the fateful step involved my girlfriend.

By this stage my girlfriend is also the mother of our two children. This is the fall of 1993. Our younger daughter is a few weeks old.

I say "fall" rather than "autumn" because the four of us are in the United States, on holiday in the Great Smoky Mountains at the junction of North Carolina and Tennessee. I am pleased to discover that this is Roosevelt country. The small house we have rented is a leftover from the Tennessee Valley Authority. In these woods, huts were built to house the workers who built the dams that contributed so greatly to the recovery of the United States's economy during the 1930s.

The dams soar to impenetrable heights above great rivers. They shoot great peacock plumes of water into the dawn air. The plumes make rainbows against the dams' sheer faces. We can feel the earth throb.

It is a beautiful part of the world. There are bears in the woods and the leaves are just beginning to turn. Paths dwindle down hillsides and through dappled light. We skip pebbles across clear green water.

One day we take a train ride on the Great Smoky Mountain Railroad. It promises to transport us back in time. In fact it transports us along the southern edge of the mountainsides. Through the window we can see wisps of mist rising from the mountains. The morning mist burns off as the sun peers from behind shrouded hills.

Despite the beauty, one of our children is fractious and seemingly inconsolable. She has recently fallen from a horse. Her lip is cut and swollen and a tooth is missing.

In the seat opposite us is an old man.

He smiles at our daughter. Spread out on the table are teacups and spoons. He takes a spoon, tarnished with generations of tannin. He spits on it.

By spitting on it he engages our daughter's attention. In her experience old people do not spit. In her experience old people, which is to say her parents, wipe up her spit with an exasperated air and pursed lips. With first his tie and then his shirttail the old man begins to polish the spoon. He worries at it. He works away at the tannin residue. From the brown forgotten spoon emerges a bright and shining mirror. He holds it up to my daughter's face. In the concave surface her face looks crushed and funny, and she gives a gap-toothed grin. The old man turns the spoon over, and this time she giggles. Now her face is long. Her nose has disappeared. The gap has gone.

The old man has a kind face. His laughter lines tug at his ears. He wears woollen trousers and leather shoes, and he tells us he is from Switzerland but now lives in Florida. While he plays with our daughter he talks to us about being an immigrant to the United States. He is of the view that the United States suffers from its inability to tell true stories about itself. "Americans have forgotten where they come from," he says. "They have forgotten what it means to suffer."

Earlier, in Philadelphia, my girlfriend's father and I worked out my daughter's "bloodlines." We limited ourselves to three generations, on the basis of which we decided she is a quarter English, a quarter Scots, one-eighth Irish, one-eighth Norwegian, three-sixteenths Welsh, and one-sixteenth French. Perhaps, since her parents are South African, she is South African. Perhaps, since she was born in London, she is English. Perhaps identity is not a matter of memory at all, and the Americans are right. Perhaps we *can* choose who to be.

On the train in the mountains the old Swiss émigré and my daughter start on a second spoon. They take turns to spit and to rub. They giggle when saliva dribbles onto the Formica tabletop. By the end of the journey they have a line of bright and shining spoons. They hold them up to each other, to see their reflections.

My daughter's tears are forgotten.

The old man has a heavy accent and a moustache. Before he started the game with the spoons he was doing the crossword in the *New York Times*. He wishes us well with our holiday. He doffs his hat to my daughter.

"Never forget," he says, "that with spit and patience you can fix anything."

It is Indian summer in the Great Smoky Mountains. In the evening we barbecue spare ribs. While sweet pinewood smoke curls around us we try an old crossword. It is also from the (London) *Guardian*. It is by a setter calling himself Araucaria. At this stage I have no idea who Araucaria is, nor that he is so popular.

In due course I will learn. Several setters, indeed, quote him as the reason they took it up the first place. Hornblower, for example, remembers an epiphany on Mykonos in 1969 when he was doing an Araucaria clue that had "Buckfastleigh" as an answer. The thirteen across solutions each started with one of the letters that make up Buckfastleigh, which is the longest English place name with no repeated letters. He was so taken with the artistry of this clue, with the beauty and patience of the thought behind it, that he started to set puzzles himself. Other setters have other epiphanies. Shed, although a big fan of Araucaria, dates his beginning from when he managed to solve a clue by Bunthorne. He was predisposed to like them though. Both he and his mother set puzzles for the *Guardian*.

Clues like the one for Buckfastleigh come from a grand tradition. Queen Victoria is reputed to have been a keen puzzler and setter (and solver) of acrostics. She is supposed to have invented one for her children to solve in which there were nine clues. The first letter of each answer, taken in order, spelled out the name of an English town. The last letter of each, again taken in reverse order, spelled out what that town is known for.[10]

Hornblower is not alone. Another eminent setter, who calls himself Enigmatist in the *Guardian* and who grew up doing puzzles in the *Telegraph* and *Daily Mail* with his parents, became a convert to the *Guardian* when he solved a clue by Araucaria in 1978. He wrote to Araucaria, and the relationship blossomed. Enigmatist became the youngest winner ever of the *Times* Crossword Competition, and also the youngest broadsheet setter ever. In 2000, Araucaria returned his original letter to him.

My girlfriend is not a bad solver. She has an instinct for the answer. Some solvers find the constituent parts first. My girlfriend finds the answer first, and then works out why. She has a way of getting at the hidden meanings that escape me.

I do not remember any clues from this particular puzzle. But I do remember how the cold night settled on the woods. I remember how our daughters fell asleep. And I remember how my girlfriend and I worked our way slowly, with spit and patience, through that crossword until only a few clues remained unsolved. I remember how we worried at it and how different clues threw up memories for each of us. I remember how we would smile in sudden recognition, how our eyes caught us each in the other's embrace. I remembered how we made up the rules. My girlfriend in fact knows quite a few of the rules, and some of the conventions too. She teaches me that in a crossword clue "sailor" can mean "AB" (as in Able-Bodied seaman) or "TAR" or "SALT" and that "worker" will often mean "ANT."

I remember her doodles around the edge of the puzzle. They grow organically. Like little seeds, they flower and blossom.

To watch my girlfriend doodle is to watch a time-lapse film of a flower. The seed breaks, and the flower begins to push its way through the soil. The slender stem of the flower brushes aside dark clods of earth. The not-as-yet-green stem reaches the crust of the earth and breaks through. On seeing the sun, it speeds its growth. Leaves appear, and petals. The flower opens. From nowhere an orchestra arrives. There is music and color. Sometimes in my girlfriend's doodles the flower becomes a fireworks display. Bright lights burst against a city landscape. They burn themselves out and fall to earth. They are the seeds of the next generation of flowers.

At this moment I am completely in love.

In 1993 my girlfriend and I sat in the quiet of a Smoky Mountain night and did an Araucaria puzzle in the *Guardian*.

I remember the warm glow in which we basked.

The next day I wanted to do it again.

I had critical mass.

moscow
rules

I could have walked away from crosswords.

But I didn't.

I could have been South African.

But I'm not.

In my mind these two processes are inextricably linked.

In the spring of 1994 I traveled to Moscow in pursuit of a story
for the BBC. It was not my first visit.

My first time in Moscow was a decade earlier, when my girlfriend and I flew from Nairobi to Athens. We had been unable
to travel, as we had hoped, through Uganda, Ethiopia, or the
Sudan, all of which were embroiled in ugly civil wars. As it hap-

pened, the cheapest flight from Nairobi to Athens was with
Aeroflot, which meant that we had to travel via Moscow. I appreciate that this is the long way around.

As it happens, we were keen to visit Moscow.

For young South Africans in the spring of 1984, Moscow
was the heart of a huge, forbidden world. My girlfriend and I
were curious to know what it was like in this forbidden world.
We were curious to know what the Soviet Union looked like.
So we flew from Nairobi to Moscow through the night and arrived in a cold and foggy Sheremet'evo airport on May Day.

Since our flight involved a two-day layover in Moscow, we
were told that Intourist would provide us with a free tour of
the city. We were told, in Nairobi, that we would see Red
Square.

To us it did not seem probable. It did not even seem possible.

But the woman from Aeroflot who sold us the tickets
seemed to think it was certain.

CUT TO:

*A travel agency in an African city. From behind a table a
brightly dressed and made-up woman with blond hair is speaking to two suntanned travelers, a young man and a young
woman. The travelers do not look like they have two pennies
to rub together. The blonde speaks through vermilion lips,
with a strong Russian accent.*

BLOND WOMAN: You will like Red Square. Everyone likes
  Red Square.

TRAVELING MAN: Are you from Moscow?

BW: No, I am from Omsk.

TRAVELING WOMAN: But you have been to Moscow?

BW: I have been to Moscow.

TW: To Red Square?

BW: To Red Square.

TM: Wow.

TW: Why will we like it?

BW: You will like everything about the Soviet Union.

"Vermilion" is another word that strikes a chord when it
turns up in a crossword puzzle some years later. "Obnoxious
creatures primed with lubricant turning bright scarlet (9)."[11]

Mmmm. Not a pretty sight, but legitimate, a bit like a
scrambled goal.

Armed with these promises, my girlfriend and I board the flight
in Nairobi with mounting excitement and wait impatiently
through the night to see Moscow, and Red Square. I remember
sitting on the airport tarmac in Cairo, watching the airport
lights, and thinking how unlikely it was that I should be flying
to the Soviet Union. I tried to dredge up images of Moscow, but
nothing came to mind. Some years later I found myself in a
house in Johannesburg having dinner with a man who is now
an eminent member of the South African government.

This is in 1990, soon after the African National Congress and the South African Communist Party were unbanned. It is a very difficult time for the leadership of the African National Congress. They have come "home," but home is a different and threatening place. "Third force" elements are wreaking havoc on commuter trains around Johannesburg. There is political violence on all fronts. It is not certain at all that the government is sincere in its desire to create a democracy.

My companion has been in exile for more than thirty years. "I tried to make a call from a call box," he says, "but I didn't know what it would look like. I was standing on the corner of Eloff and Market, and I didn't know what to look for. I had to ask a taxi driver!"

My companion warms to his theme.

"How can this be?" he says. "In New York and London and Moscow I know what the phone boxes look like. But here I am at 'home,' and I don't know."

"It's been a long ride," I said. I am trying to picture a South African phone box. Like my companion, I can visualize them in London and New York, but not in Johannesburg. Unlike him, I am not troubled by this. I have no intention of living there.

"A long ride," he repeated. "And it's not over yet."

On the flight to Moscow in 1984 I squeeze my girlfriend's hand, but she is asleep. She seems less surprised than I am that we should be flying to Moscow.

But we land to crushing disappointment. What the lady with the vermilion lipstick in Nairobi had not calculated was that we would land in Moscow on May Day, and that this would be Intourist's busiest day of the year. On the day we arrived, they were so busy, in fact, that the promised visit to Red Square was not forthcoming.

In fact, nothing was forthcoming. The guides were busy, and our papers were not in order.

We were please to come this way.

We came this way, and armed men in uniform took our passports and sent us under armed guard to a hotel on the airport perimeter, where they escorted us to a room and locked us in. From the window it was possible to see a small stand of silver birch trees, where the frost lay in the shadows all day.

We stayed there for thirty-six hours, eating borscht and Vienna schnitzel and wondering what, exactly, Red Square looked like. From time to time we would attempt to wander about the hotel, but soldiers with guns would bid us desist.

"*Nyet*," they said. "*Nyet.*"

"It probably means desist," said my girlfriend.

"Yes, I mean, no," I agreed.

And then they put us on another airplane, and we flew to Athens.

Ten years later, almost to the day, I am in Moscow for the second time. This time my papers are in order. I have brought with me three pieces of identity.

I have my British passport.

I have my South African identity document.

And I have the second anthology of *Guardian* crosswords.

On the flight to Moscow, I come across a clue. "The doctors are intimidating around the Kremlin (6)." I do not know whose clue this is. The anthology dates from the time when *Guardian* setters still had their anonymity. Shortly after this anthology was published, John Perkin, who edited the *Guardian* crossword for thirty-eight years, introduced pseudonyms. He called them "both a warning and a promise." As you got to know a setter's style, you got to know also whether you wanted to bother with his puzzles.

At first this clue troubles me. I have learned that "doctor" is often "DR" and that "doctors" therefore are presumably "DRS." Which must be put next to a word for "intimidating" to give an answer that may be found around the Kremlin.

It is only as we come in to land that I let myself peek at the answer: MOSCOW.

Doctors can also be Medical OfficerS.

"Be intimidating" is "cow." "Cow" does not, in this instance, mean a milk-producing bovine quadruped.

Moscow is around the Kremlin.

I've heard that one before.

But I do get it.

Moscow.

.   .   .

Ostensibly my companion and I are in Moscow to research matters to do with the Romanov archive, and to acquire rights to exploit that archive on the television screens of the world.

Ostensibly.

I have another agenda. It is to vote in South Africa's first democratic elections.

I have checked, and I know that, like thousands of South Africans around the world, I can do this at the newly opened South African embassy. I have a friend who lives in Moscow. On the morning in question she takes me to the South African embassy, where I present myself and collect my ballot papers, which I receive on presentation of my South African identity document. It is a small green book with a photograph of me the year I left Cape Town. I was considerably better-looking then than I am now.

The identity document gives my address as Somerset Road, Cape Town. It says I own no firearms, and that I am single. It says I voted in the constitutional referendum of 1983,[12] and that I am licensed to drive a car and a motorcycle.

It describes who I was, not who I am.

In South Africa's first democratic elections there were two votes: a national vote and a provincial vote. I am allowed to choose which province. I am allowed to choose who I am. The South African ambassador himself is there to assist. The ambassador himself is of the old guard, although he is new to this post.

"So where are you from?" he asks.

My girlfriend and I have caucused this in London. My girlfriend has come from that generation of South African activists for whom it goes without saying that there will be a pre-caucus caucus. In the pre-caucus caucus the inner circle will decide the outcome of the caucus.

It is a question, usually, of tactics.

In the case of the first South African elections, it is a tactical question of where the most votes are needed.

"Cape Town," I say.

You will know that this is not strictly true. I was born in Johannesburg, grew up near Durban, and had lived the past ten years in London.

But tactically speaking, I am from Cape Town. I am from Cape Town because it seems that the Western Cape is the province where the African National Congress is least certain to win control. I want the African National Congress to win control. And so I vote in the Western Cape, and the ambassador helps me stuff my papers into the ballot box.

Since I am also a journalist, I ask him how many other people have voted in the South African elections in Moscow.

He is surprisingly precise.

"Twenty-five," he says.

"Twenty-five?"

"Ja."

"And why are they all here? I mean, what are these South Africans doing in a place like Moscow?"

I had expected him to say they are all exiles completing their studies. I had expected him to say they are all ANC people.

What he said was this.

"Ag, there's only two reasons we come here, hey. Guns or diamonds. These guys are all doing guns or diamonds. And what's your line of business?"

"Diamonds," I say, opting for the safer of the two identities on offer.

That vote was on a Tuesday. Those of us who voted in embassies and consulates around the world voted before the people "at home." The people in South Africa voted on the Thursday and the Friday of the same week.

Since I was in Moscow, I did not see the *Guardian* that week, and so I did not know that Araucaria set a puzzle to mark the occasion of South Africa's first democratic elections. It was puzzle number 20014, and according to the preamble it was "A tribute on election day to the fighters for democracy, especially martyrs such as 6, 16 and 3." Six, 16, and 3 were Ruth First, Steve Biko, and Chris Hani, all great leaders murdered in the course of the struggle for national liberation. Other heroes of this particular struggle who found their way into the puzzle were Alan Paton, and Helen Joseph and Joe Slovo (who, touchingly I thought, shared a clue). Then there was the triumvirate who more than any others transformed the African National Congress from the voice of plaintive nationalism to the mass movement it became, and the party of government it now is: Nelson Mandela, Walter Sisulu, and the late Oliver Tambo. There was also space for Cyril Ramaphosa, who led the often dramatic, sometimes tedious, but ultimately triumphant negotiations that led to the creation of the new democracy.

The idea for the puzzle came to Araucaria quite late, and he had to telephone John Perkin, the editor, and ask him, as it were, to hold the back page for a "special." Perkin remembered the moment vividly, and was able to tell me both the puzzle number and that Araucaria had used *Guardian* grid number 40. Recently I asked Araucaria about why he did it, and his answer was typically direct. "These were people I thought *Guardian* readers should know," he said.

He said this with strength and conviction, with the moral force of his life as a priest, and with a hint of anger, and it was only afterward that it occurred to me that "should" in this context can have more than one meaning.

That a crossword compiler should assert a moral obligation on the part of his solvers struck me as remarkable. That the obligation should be to be engaged with international causes sufficiently to know the names of a variety of leading figures brought a tear to my eye. It reminded me of the much-quoted wish of Louis MacNeice. "I would have a poet able-bodied, fond of talking, a reader of the newspapers, capable of pity and laughter, informed in economics, appreciative of women, involved in personal relationships, actively interested in politics, susceptible to physical impressions . . ."

And a solver, I like to think, of crossword puzzles.

. . .

On Tuesday, after I voted in Moscow, I went to dinner with my friend, who lived in a tower block some distance out of town. Her husband is a journalist, and is in Tblisi.

Her husband is often in places like Tblisi. Or Yerevan. Or Baku.

Many years later I see his byline on reports from Belgrade. At the time he is in Belgrade the Americans and the British are bombing large parts of Serbia. The parts of Belgrade bombed include the television tower and the Chinese embassy.

There are no rules, for this sort of thing.

"How was it?" my friend asks, offering me fresh bread. She is referring to the voting, but she is also happy because there is a bakery on the road opposite the new South African embassy in Moscow, and while I voted she considered herself lucky to find fresh bread.

This is, after all, 1994. Shortages are common in Russia, and bakeries do not always have flour.

"It was fantastic," I reply. "Really extraordinary."

And it was, but somewhere inside I feel like a fraud, because it is not really my vote, and no longer my country. I live in London, remember, and have two English daughters.

"This is good bread," I add.

. . .

The rest of the week in Moscow passes swiftly. At the State
Archive of the Russian Federation the director lets us loose on
his precious history. One night he shows me the love letters of
Nicholas and Alexandra. There are menus from parties they
held, and boxes of photographs.

Another time he shows me a box containing a piece of
Hitler's skull and the documentation to prove it. I spend two
days with a translator working through the correspondence between Beria, Stalin, and Molotov. There is some debate as to
what they should or should not admit to the Allies. They agree
to lie; they consider that it is in their interests that the Allies
should be unsure whether or not Hitler is dead. Together with
the correspondence and the piece of skull are six volumes of
transcripts of interrogations of those who were with Hitler in
his bunker in March and April of 1945, including hand-drawn
maps of "who slept where."

The director of the State Archive organizes for me a tour of
the Kremlin. We stand in Red Square. Outside a Georgian restaurant I buy watercolors for five dollars each. When I get them
framed in London it costs me £85.

In a courtyard at the State Archive, trucks arrive and tip
huge mounds of books and papers onto the ground. The director shakes his head. "What do I do with all this?" he asks.
"What do I do?"

"All this" means files and documents he is being sent by the
KGB. Ten years after Gorbachev invented glasnost, the KGB
are practicing it. They are sending old files to the State Archive,
but they are doing it without explanation, and there is some-

thing menacing about the volume of files, and the way they arrive without warning.

The director does not know what to do. He is not sure what, as it were, lurks beneath. He is not sure who is pulling which strings.

He smells a rat.

Moscow at this time is full of rats.

But he cannot resist the files. He picks one up at random from the ground and brushes it free of dirt and dust. He flips through it. He has an air of wonder about him, and of repressed delight.

"These are some stories," he says, shaking his head. "Some stories." The director of the State Archive strikes me as a kind of hero.

Years later I was reminded of this by Enigmatist from the *Guardian*, who told me this clue: "The real reason for the meeting of Volkswagen and Daimler (6,6)."

I look at this clue blankly for several minutes. The answer, he told me, is HIDDEN AGENDA, which is "the real reason," but which remains hidden until you put Volksw**AGEN/ DA**imler together.

It was when he told me this clue that I realized I had some way to go as a solver. Some time later the clue appeared in one of his puzzles in the *Guardian*. Unfortunately I was doing the puzzle on my own, and was unable to impress my girlfriend.

. . .

Later that night in Moscow, Euronews is carrying feeds of the voting in South Africa. The images switch randomly. One moment we are in Sandton, the next in Guguletu. I am testing myself to see if I can name each place, before the caption comes up. Thokoza and Glenwood, Nelspruit and Kwamashu. I remember being in Soweto in 1990, when Mandela first went there after his release. I remember the man who smiled for our camera. "Like magic," he said, wiping away a tear. On the television screen, maids and madams queue, and just for a day the maids are winning.

At the same time I have one eye on my book of *Guardian* crosswords. I am pleased to solve "Hires TV and does well out of it (7)."* But I can't get "Queen ceases to rule in Rhodesia (8,5)."

Rhodesia?

I do what anyone would have done. I phone my girlfriend, who at that moment is also watching television in our house near the Arsenal. She tells me a story about our daughter.

That afternoon there was a guest at our house. And the television was on. There were frequent images of Nelson Mandela.

*THRIVES, an anagram of "Hires TV."

"I don't like Mr. Mandela," said our three-year-old daughter.

My girlfriend was suitably mortified.

"Why not?" she asked nervously.

"He makes Mummy cry."

And it is true. Mandela makes us cry. He makes our eyes brim and our throats swell. Over the telephone line my girlfriend and I chuckle at our daughter's wisdom, but I have other concerns.

"Eight and five," I say. "Queen ceases to rule in Rhodesia?"

"I should bloody well hope so," says my girlfriend.

"No, man!" I say, lapsing into South African idiom. "It's a crossword clue."

"Oh, right."

There is a beat. I listen to the silence down thousands of miles of telephone line.

"Victoria Falls," she says.

She makes it seem so easy.

"Why Rhodesia?" she adds.

I had already thought of that, and checked.

"The collection was published in 1968," I reply, but in my mind I am seeing the way she brushes her hair from her forehead.

And so that night, all through the night, I lie in my hotel room and watch the silent television images of the voting queues in South Africa, watch soundlessly as the faces of my childhood wind their way to the voting booths, watch silently and alone as history has its day.

And when, finally, I fall asleep in a hotel room in Moscow, it is with these images in my mind and a book of *Guardian* crosswords crushed beneath my cheek.

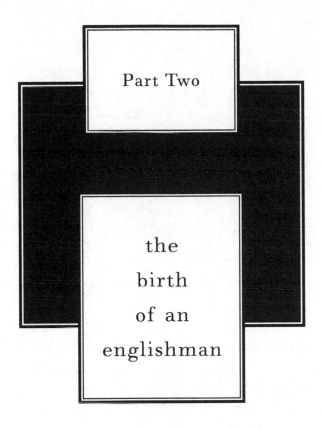

Part Two

the
birth
of an
englishman

potty
training

It is seven-thirty on a clear morning in the spring of 1995 and my girlfriend is in denial. There is something epic about her refusal to countenance the obvious. In her stubbornness she reminds me of those posters from the early years of the Soviet Union, where the women fix tractors and build guns. The women in these posters are strong; their hair is tied back and their eyes are set on a distant prize. They appear largely to ignore the men around them. My girlfriend at this moment has the strong jaw and fixed look of a woman on a Soviet poster. She ignores me.

It is my view that this is not entirely appropriate, but I say nothing.

.   .   .

Some years later, a setter for the *Guardian* tells me that "I say nothing (3)"* is the perfect crossword clue. I am inclined to agree. As it happens, it is also the perfect response to my girlfriend.

The matter about which my girlfriend was in denial in the spring of 1995 was the imminent birth of our third child. On this particular morning she does not believe the midwife, who has just said that my girlfriend is 8 centimeters dilated and that if we want the child to be born in a hospital we had better get going now.

"I don't think so," says my girlfriend, recalling the births of our two daughters. "I always take forever." As it happens, we have a clear idea of how long "forever" is. My girlfriend was in labor for twenty-seven hours for the first child and twelve hours for the second. She sees no reason to think the third will be any quicker.

For me this is a delicate political problem. Every instinct tells me I should listen to the midwife. She sounds like she knows what she is talking about. She has a confident air and a homely manner. She has done this many times before. She is the sort of midwife who is relaxed enough to recommend Guinness to pregnant women. Midwives who have, as it were, been around the block a few times are happy to recommend

---

*EGO, a synonym for "I," where "eg" is "say" and O is "nothing." Concise, exact, full of narrative potential; brilliant.

Guinness. They do this not because Guinness contains alcohol, but because it contains iron. Midwives who have been less often around the block are more inclined to recommend vitamin tablets with iron supplements. Since this is our third child, and we might ourselves therefore be thought to have gone around the block more than once, my girlfriend has gone with the Guinness.

At the off-license on Blackstock Road a few weeks earlier I bought a case of Guinness.

"It's for my girlfriend," I said. "She's pregnant. The midwife recommended it. For the iron."

"Ah, that'll be Sister Mary," said the man at the counter.

"I have done this many times before," says Sister Mary. "We've got maybe thirty minutes."

My girlfriend grunts and looks the other way.

"Twelve hours, minimum," she says.

Denial is triumphing over experience.

I realize that this is not a situation in which science holds sway. We are dealing here with the prerogative of millennia. If my girlfriend says she is not giving birth, then she is not giving birth. It is as simple as that. No amount of broken waters, contractions, or dilation can alter this. She wonders out loud whether she should go into the office.

"After all," she says, "nothing will happen between now and supper."

It is seven twenty-eight in the morning. The midwife and I

exchange glances across the room. We are upstairs at my girl-friend's and my house near the Arsenal. A friend is downstairs getting ready to take the girls to their nursery school. On the wall above our bed is a portrait of my girlfriend painted by a friend of hers from Cape Town. It shows a blond shape with beady eyes and a splash of crimson.

"Sweetie . . ." I begin, but a single glance from those beady eyes shuts me up.

"Give me five minutes," says the midwife. I realize I am ban-ished and go downstairs to say goodbye to the girls. Then I sit in our sitting room and idly pick up a copy of the paper. I have not yet attempted this crossword. I look at it without much interest, but a clue catches my eye. It is in the first puzzle by a new setter who calls himself Paul.

"Potty train (4)."

It seems peculiarly apt. I know all about potty training. Our second daughter is still in diapers, but the elder is now master— or is that mistress?—of her own elaborate toilet habit. Getting there has taught me more than I ever wish to know about the workings of the human bowel. The experience of having two children has also taught me the exact equivalence between the child benefit paid to parents by the British state and the cost of disposable diapers. Each week since 1991 we have taken our child benefit and given it to the supermarkets who, in turn, have given us diapers. I suspect this is not the equation the gov-ernment had in mind when it created child benefit, but it is the one that works for us.

I think about the child about to be born. We do not know its sex. Secretly, since we have two girls, I am hoping for a boy. Outwardly, though, I am indifferent. For some weeks we have been scouring the name books. There is the delicate question of how much homage to pay to our respective families. We find choosing girls' names easier, perhaps because we have been there twice before. Part of the fun of looking up names is to discover hitherto only dimly understood meanings. My name— Alexander—is sometimes translated as "savior of mankind" or "defender of men." It seems terribly unlikely. But heroic. Unquestionably this is a heroic name. Alexander the Great made sure of that. The diminutive is marginally less heroic. "Little boy that hasn't got shingles? (5)" is hardly a flattering rendition of "Sandy."

Potty train.

Four letters.

It is a classic of the "double lit." formation, which is to say that the solution is a synonym for both parts of the clue. We need a word that means both "train" and "potty." But the particular brilliance of the clue is that it is very difficult to separate these two words from each other because together they are such a specific phrase, with such specific associations.

Many years later I come across a similar example, culled from an Internet message board dedicated to crossword puzzles. "Wipe bum (6)." This is also a "double lit." It requires a word that means both "wipe" and "bum." But again the surface meaning is so compelling that it takes an act of will to ignore that and to think instead of a word that might mean both. The answer in this case is "sponge," for which we have to accept that "bum" is a legitimate American phrase for "to cadge."

"Wipe bum" is a beautiful clue for "sponge." Elegant, concise, legitimate. It is, for example, considerably more elegant and concise than another clue for the same word like "Sulphur's the bad smell Oriental found in the bathroom (6)."[13]

Both are legitimate clues (although one might query the apostrophe-S of "Sulphur's"), but only one has a place in anyone's list of favorites. In discussing clues, many people use the same sort of criteria listed above. First of all it must have good surface. The clue, when read straight, must say something clear and simple. It should be the sort of phrase that triggers memories or thoughts, or that extracts an emotional response. It must have all or some of many qualities. Precision, concision, legitimacy, humor. It must say what it means, but it need not mean what it says.

But as I engage with crosswords I have come around to the view that the key to a truly great crossword clue is narrative. Does it either tell, or enable others to tell, a story? Does it release a flood of memory? Does it have layers? Is it a peach? Many years later, in a decent enough pub near Vauxhall, an eminent setter tells me that this is the rule. "There should be," he says, "at least one peach per puzzle." A peach is a clue that causes solvers to sigh with satisfaction, either because they are so clever to have got it, or, preferably, because the clue itself is very clever.

A clever clue is not necessarily hard to solve.

Potty train?

I hear noises upstairs. The midwife and my girlfriend are coming down. I get up to help.

"We must hurry," says the midwife "She's pretty much fully dilated."

"Do you have other people you need to see?" says my girlfriend, "Because I'm fine."

She is still, it seems, in denial.

I grab the bag we have prepared to take to the hospital. Bitter experience—which is to say, twenty-seven hours without coffee when our first child was born—has taught me that it is better to be overprepared, so I have packed a suitcase that contains enough food and clothing to see three or four adults through a Siberian winter. We move in convoy out to our car. My girlfriend is moaning conspicuously.

"How are you feeling?" I ask.

I need not tell you that this is not a helpful intervention.

She climbs into the backseat of the car. She is under instruction from the midwife to keep her head down and her backside up.

"We don't want baby coming out just yet, do we, dear?" she says.

Baby?

Midwives, in my experience, do talk like this. They are keen not to presume as to the sex of the child, but nor do they want to refer to it as "it."

I climb in the front and we set off. Only then do I realize I am still clutching the newspaper.

Potty train (4)?

It nags at me.

Perhaps it is a quality of double literals. Either you get them straight away, or you're lost. "Go round (4)," for example, cropped up in the *Guardian* recently. So did "Distort time (7)" and "Tarry rope" (4).*

It is rush hour. The midweek streets of north London are clogged with cars. We inch our way up the Stroud Green Road, and turn left on Tollington Park. On the backseat my girlfriend seems to have achieved a certain kind of peace. She is on her hands and knees. She closes her eyes and breathes through the pain. With her face pressed to the seat and her bottom covering the window, she cannot see what I see. What I see is the curious looks of passersby. What I can see is the truck reversing into the

---

*SHOT, STRETCH, and STAY, by Araucaria, Paul, and Hendra, respectively. These can be extended a little, on a setter's whim. "Mad, passionate lovers (7)," for example, was set by Spurius in the *Independent*. Since Spurius is both a setter and his own editor, he is perhaps allowed a little leniency. The answer, of course, is BONKERS.

path of the oncoming bus. Although the resulting jam takes only minutes to clear, it seems to last forever.

What I can see is also the London of terraced streets that I remember from when I first arrived in the city in the early summer of 1984. It seemed to me now that I had come a long way. I remembered my parents' stories of the same process, when I was born in Johannesburg, in the Marymount Maternity Clinic. My father drove this same journey through the streets of Johannesburg. At the time I was born, Johannesburg probably did not know what a traffic jam looked like.

By this time I have lived almost eleven years in London. My work takes me to distant and exotic countries, from which I return "home" to a terraced house indistinguishable from all the other terraced houses around it. As we drive to the hospital I reflect that I don't need to put home in quotes. Our house is my home, and these people are my life. Coming home is my favorite journey. I can't count the number of times I have sat, half asleep, on the Tube from Heathrow airport, feeling the rhythms of the train, watching the ebb and flow of passengers climbing on and off, and taking a gentle pleasure from the familiarity of the way the people look.

On this particular morning in the spring of 1995 there is a dreamlike quality to the houses and shops of the Stroud Green Road. The gray and brown hues of Victorian London are broken by occasional flashes of daffodil and tulip. We are going against the flow of pedestrians as they make their way to Finsbury Park. They are winter leaves in a fast-flowing stream.

Sealed in our car, with time seemingly still, we are like a salmon come to spawn. Not far to go now, the salmon pauses and holds itself against the flow. The spring melt swirls past it and, tired and drained, it seems that in a moment it will be swept downstream. But with a single flick of its tail it starts to move upstream again. What must be, must be. We cannot resist the call.

Ahead of us the traffic clears, and I pull away.

"Aaaagh," says my girlfriend as another set of contractions consumes her.

"Be there soon," I promise. "Looks like the midwife was right. You're going to pop any minute.

"What do you think," I add. "Four letters, 'potty train'?"

"Aaaagh," says my girlfriend.

"Gosh," I reply, "They're coming thick and fast now."

"That. Wasn't. A. Contraction," says my girlfriend. "I must be mad to do this again," she adds.

Mad? Of course! The answer to "Potty train (4)" is "loco," which can mean both "mad" and a "train."

I look in the mirror to make sure the midwife is staying close behind.

Births, in their way, are violent affairs. But for all the violence and the mess and the pain, it is impossible to forget the fragile beauty of the moment the child clenches its eyes against the light and lets rip a yell nine months in the making.

Ten minutes after we reached the north London hospital on a spring day in 1995, my girlfriend gave birth to our third child. He has a squashed face, and hungry lips, and his fingers are perfectly manicured. I remember handing him to my girlfriend with tears in my eyes.

"It's a boy," I said.

It could have been me.

betwixt
and
between

We get home to find that our house, and several other houses in the street, have been burgled. All that has been taken from ours is the bag for my laptop. Fortunately the laptop was not in the bag at the time. It turns out that the only item of value in it was my South African identity document.

"You can always get it replaced," says my girlfriend.

This is true, but I am not so sure I want to. The new South African government has decided to take fingerprints of everyone applying for driver's licenses, identity documents, passports, and the like. For some reason I find this deeply offensive.

"I liked the photograph," I say. "I liked being twenty-one. I had hair."

But I know that she is right. I can always get it replaced, though this is not the sort of answer I am looking for.

.   .   .

The first trick to solving a clue is to decide what sort of answer you are looking for. Does it mean or describe the first phrase or the last? Is it some other variation?

The second trick is to decide what sort of clue it is. Find the story that best fits the available evidence.

There are—depending which how-to book you read—perhaps eight distinct kinds of crossword clue. Anagrams, and their variations, are one kind. Double literals, like "Potty train (4)" or "Wipe bum (6)," are another. Each clue presents itself to the solver, and the task of the solver is then to find the clue type that works, to find the story that best fits the clue.

Within any given puzzle this should not be too difficult. Any given puzzle should have a few examples of all or most types of clue. This is what editors do. An editor on a broadsheet paper in Britain will reject or alter a puzzle that has, for example, too many "double lits." And so, if only by a process of elimination, it becomes possible to work out what type of clue each is. But solving a puzzle is not simply a technical process. To understand and solve crosswords it is necessary to understand the stories hidden within the clues.

But it is best to start with the simple questions. Is it an anagram? If not, is it a double literal? If not a double lit, then what? Perhaps it is a reversal, in which words or letters or phrases have to be read backward if the clue is to be solved. Perhaps things are tripping back on themselves.

Perhaps the world is upside down.

Speaking of which, it is my second spring of 1995.

For all that I was building a life in London, I remained insatiably curious about what it was I had left behind. It is as much out of curiosity as anything else that my girlfriend and I and our three English children have come, temporarily, to live in Cape Town, and by October the weather is warm and the land is beautiful. The winter rains have been reasonable; life is thrusting its way from the earth. For us the warm summer in England has given way to an even warmer Cape October. The rains of June and July are over; the winds of August and September have passed on. October is a lovely time to be in Cape Town.

Our third child was born in the northern spring. Now six months old, he is using his second spring to discover the nutritional properties of beach sand. His sisters are more interested in noodles, sun, and water. We have taken a house in St. James, where there is a tidal pool and a small beach. The distant mountains sit easily in the ocean haze. From our bedroom we look over the calm waters of False Bay. The bay got its name early during the European period of expansionism. Sailors rounding Cape Point would assume they had passed the southernmost tip of Africa. But as they hugged the coast, they would soon find themselves once again heading south. The bay is real enough; the hope it presents the weary mariner is false.

It occurs to me that False Bay would work well in a crossword puzzle. It is not hard to imagine the ways in which one could clue it, although any such clue would probably only work in a

South African context. There is no reasonable expectation that others have heard of False Bay. I realize that to have an involvement with crosswords is to spend at least some of one's time imaging how words might be clued. Much later, for example, I am in a pub in north London in the company of some crossword people, and two setters are joking at the delight they take in London place names.

"It's impossible to walk around this town," exclaims one. "The names are too much fun. Every bloody corner offers a name just begging to be clued."

He sips his pint reflectively. I see that the rest of the table has gone quiet. The other setters sense a joke coming.

"Imagine," he continues, "what you could do with Turnham Green."

By this time even I can imagine what can be done with Turnham Green. I do not have to be Dr. Seuss to understand the various ways in which ham might be made envious.

The same is true of so many London names. Think of the Queen on the run in Lambeth. Or the advice given to the road engineers of Camberwell. Or the sound of hardened bells in Tuffnell Park, which incidentally, is not so far from where Charles II built a villa for his hard-sounding mistress. Even "park" can be clued so many ways. Is it an average king? A silent boat? Or an anagram of what's left when you delouse the loudspeaker?*

---

*Average king = PAR (golfing average) + K for King; silent boat = P + ark; take the letters of "delouse" out of "loudspeaker" and you're left with "pakr"—a suitable anagram indicator will, of course, turn this into "park."

"Or Mount Pleasant," says another setter[14] that day in the pub. Mount Pleasant. One can imagine what to do with Mount Pleasant. "Mount" is one of those deliciously ambiguous words in English. It appeared in a particularly brilliant construction in a puzzle published in the *Guardian* to mark the eightieth birthday of Araucaria, perhaps its most brilliant (and enduring) setter. The clue was "Mount Rushmore! (3-2)."*

FADE IN. *A true story:*

Two crossword setters sit in a pub in Clerkenwell and laugh. There are puns even in the way they catch each other's eyes. You can tell from their body language they have known each other a long time.

PAUL *(for it is he):* I had a job once, in a laboratory. I had to take urine samples.
    Pause.
PAUL: I was the official piss-taker.
ENIGMATIST *(for it is he):* You never told me that! I never knew that.
    Brief pause.
    A slow grin spreads over Enigmatist's face.

ENIGMATIST: Urine trouble now.
PAUL *(ruefully):* This one could run and run.

*GEE-UP.

ENIGMATIST: Aahh, look, you're all flushed. Can I get you
    something to relieve you?

PAUL: I need the loo.

ENIGMATIST: Was it something I said?

I watch as the laughter surges up the table like a wave up the
shore, turning the well-worn pebbles of these stories, washing
them afresh. I watch as each face lights up, each pun throws the
net of shared knowledge, of shared history farther. I watch as a
shared appreciation of who we are folds the group in its embrace.

As I watch I realize that these waters have broken over me
too, that I get the joke and the possibilities. I realize I am in the
company of people for whom every word is pregnant with possibility; people for whom the invisible web of words that binds all
knowledge is something real and tangible. I realize that these
are people who have climbed this web, who have followed its
threads beyond their safety limits. These are people for whom
to take a different approach is the norm. These are people who
habitually find new meanings, and reinvigorate old ones.

The crossword setters in the pub in north London are people
who have for many years—in some cases more than half a century—entertained and delighted a worldwide readership. They
tell great stories about our lives, stories both so simple and so
layered, which, if we take the time, let us know who we are, just
as they let my mother's godmother know who she was, in her
house in the suburbs of Nairobi twenty years ago.

.   .   .

In the warmth of the Cape sunshine in the southern spring of 1995 I have only the smallest inkling of the narrative potential in crosswords. And besides, there are other things to distract us. We can, for example, sit in bed and watch whales cavort in the bay. We can see their barnacled bulk moving and watch with bated breath, hoping to see their great tails flip up from the water. We can look beyond them too, to where the fishing boats from Kalk Bay are heading across the choppy water to pick up on a run of *snoek*.

My girlfriend and I have come to live in Cape Town because it is as close to Johannesburg as she is prepared to live. Cape Town, in this sense, represents a compromise between London and Johannesburg. My work is in Johannesburg. Our home is in London. Cape Town will have to do.

One Sunday, therefore, I find myself driving from Cape Town to Johannesburg. I am reminded of my girlfriend's doodles. A verdant sheen has broken the earth's crust. I know that, come nightfall, the stars will burst like bright fireworks. The Karoo has starlight like all deserts have starlight. The stars feel close enough to touch. The Karoo does not, however, have a city landscape. The Karoo is flat and stretches ahead of me, seemingly forever. But it is hemmed in by mountains, and on my right, perhaps thirty miles away, I can see the low blue shapes of the Swartberg mountain range. It seems to me that all there is between us is distance. It is very familiar. I have been here before. I have traveled both ways along this road.

What happens in a reversal is this. Somewhere in the clue there will be an indicator—a word—that tells you that you have to read or think from right to left instead of left to right. Or, in the case of "down" clues, from bottom to top, instead of top to bottom. Even my eight-year-old daughter knows this.

It can, of course, be more complicated. Shed, for example, used this technique recently in this clue: "In the ballad it runs westward, ebbing and flowing (5).* There are some who would object to the clue. In an across clue, "westward" might reasonably be thought to indicate a reversal (although those of us who come from the southern hemisphere do not always equate "left" with "west"), but not in a down clue. To which the response is that the indicator tells you what to look for in the clue, not in the answer, and therefore this is acceptable. A similar example appeared last year in the *Independent on Sunday:* "Bomb falling short west of a Caribbean island (7)."† Here "west" is used to indicate "to the left of," and again this rather depends on which way up the world is.

.   .   .

*TIDAL, from "balLAD IT runs."
†GRENADA. By Quixote, November 4, 2001.

On my way to Johannesburg I stop to buy coffee in a small town called Hanover. Hanover has fallen on hard times. The main road now bypasses the town, and few people stop here for petrol or coffee. They prefer the Ultracity service stations built on the main road. The old road runs empty past closed-down shops.

At the only garage the woman makes me coffee. This is a complicated process. First she has to find the kettle. Then the water. Then the coffee. It is clear she has not done this for some time.

I need a break and wait patiently at first. But as the delay lengthens, my patience dwindles. Perhaps thirty minutes later the kettle boils. But there is a new problem. They do not have disposable cups, and since I now want to have the coffee "to go," this is a problem. She shows me the cups they have. There are some enamel ones from the fifties, a rather fine and delicate china cup, and some metal cups of the sort that I know without asking have always only been used for the workers.

I buy an enamel cup.

I take it and the coffee inside and get into the car. Watching me, unmoving, are an old white couple sitting on the *stoep* of their house. They are watching the world go by, and for the moment I appear to be the world. But I have a real sense as I put the car into gear that it is too late. The world has already passed. I am just its memory.

The reason we have come to live in South Africa, the reason I have work in Johannesburg, is to do with a marginal role I have in testing out a popular theory. The popular theory is that the public assets of the country should be used to advance the economic interests of historically disadvantaged groups.

Often this process is referred to as "black economic empowerment," and to further this project a number of black economic empowerment companies have arisen. Several have stock-exchange listings. Many have vast new offices in which secretaries provide a façade behind which telecommunications engineers install phone lines for employees who may or may not one day be in place.

The particular public asset in which I have an interest concerns the airwaves. The new South African government wishes there to be a new television station, and it has invited applications from interested parties.

The politics of this process are very complicated, but seem to involve a series of reversals. History, happily, is being turned on its head. Old capital is being excluded. Foreign capital is being limited. Banks (masquerading as new capital) are bank-rolling new black businessmen who talk of "gearing" and "taking exits offshore." In the middle of this, a number of voices are clamoring to define just what the public interest is.

I am one of those voices. I appear in public hearings and pontificate to gatherings of legislators. In the Union Buildings in Pretoria one legislator asks why he should take me seriously. I am at a loss as to how to answer this question. Partly his question was just rude, but partly he was challenging my legitimacy. He was accusing me of being foreign. That I was representing a major British broadcaster only confused the matter.

I decide to turn his question on its head. Rather than feign South Africanness, I proclaim my Englishness.

"You should take me seriously," I say, "because where I come from we have created what I regard as the world's best model for commercially funded, public service broadcasting."

"Where I come from"?

"We"?

I *have* come a long way.

It is now early December. I am driving with my companion to Mmabatho. The road ahead is lined with blue gum trees. My companion is a former lecturer in mathematics and now a senior figure in one of the premier black economic empowerment groups. We are going to meet a woman who runs a minor television station, a relic from the homeland of Bophutatswana. On the way we discuss crosswords.

My companion has only a limited interest in crosswords. Although we were born in the same month, in the same year, and within ten miles of each other, our conversations tend to conclude with a mutual shaking of heads. We shake our heads in wonder that lives that started so close together could have traveled paths so different.

My companion, for example, is very clear that he wants to be rich. It is his single overriding ambition. I, by contrast, admit to no real desire for wealth.

"That's because you have never been poor," he says. I suspect he is right.

"You must try to think of crosswords politically," I say (knowing that my use of "must" will irritate him). "Once you know your strategic objective, the rest is merely a question of tactics. The strategic objective is the definition."

My companion whoops and smacks the dashboard.

"Don't tell me what I must do," he says.

"And then," I say, "then you have to look for clue types. Look at what is really happening. In a down clue, 'up' means just that. In an across clue, 'over' can mean 'back.' Things are fluid in a crossword. It's like a conversation."

"A conversation with whom?" he asks.

"It's how we tell stories about ourselves," I say.

He laughs again.

"You guys!" he says. "When we tell stories we do it around a fire with lots of beer and a big bowl of food. But you? You do it alone with a pen and a silly grid on a newspaper."

Now that's what I call a reversal.

"Stories have many interpretations," I say in self-defense.

Back in Hanover, a couple of months earlier, I become impatient at the delay in getting my cup of coffee. I stamp out to the car. I put the mug of coffee on the dashboard and lurch forward. The coffee lurches backward. Its spills into my groin. It is very, very hot.

Screaming I leap from the car. I am wearing denim trousers and my skin is burning. I undo my buckle and strip. But as I do so I notice that the car is moving off. The road has a slight incline. With my trousers around my ankles I dive through the window and pull on the handbrake. I glance up at the old couple and see that they have not moved. I continue my striptease and go around to the trunk to find a clean pair of jeans. My dirty ones lie in the middle of the road.

Fully clothed again, and within spitting distance of my dignity, I look up at the couple. I make some modest joke at my own expense. I presume that they do not see people stripping in the main road every day. In making the joke I have assumed that their response will be one of sympathy. I assume they will have seen something amusing in the sight of my flaccid butt waggling from the window of a moving car.

But their response indicates they have seen the story in an entirely different way.

The man points to my dirty jeans lying on the road.

"Het jy dié nog nodig?" he asks. Do you still need those? It occurs to me that I had read the story from left to right. For them it was the other way around. After all, they had been poor, and still were.

wellington,
texas

In crosswords we tell stories about ourselves. But who is telling the story? It is a good idea to ask this question early on. Is it the solver, or is it the setter? Whose voice is this? Just what is the definition here? Just what is the meaning I am looking for? A good clue will send the solver shooting off into a variety of orbits, but he will always come back to the same point. After all, all that is required is that he think of a synonym for the definition. How hard can that be?

Take, for example, "Linguist and Philosopher opposed to Vietnam War writing in prison (7)," a clue that appeared in the *Guardian* early in 2002.

. . .

What does it mean? What is the definition?

It seems to me now that for too many years I have traveled the world thinking about England, thinking about why I chose to live in England, thinking about what it means to be English. As with anywhere, it is fair to say that England's welcome for foreigners will never be unqualified. It is not so long ago that one of the broadsheet newspapers criticized a fellow South African (the cricketer Tony Greig) on the grounds that "he is an Englishman by adoption and not by birth. There is a world of difference between the two."

The difference, we adopted children might say, is that we see a broader canvas. Our loyalty is an active thing; we do not have it thrust on us. We nurture it over many years.

The United States, for instance, offers a different welcome, and a well-documented one. And for some years I imagined I would, sooner or later, move to the United States. The U.S. invented the crossword and was the home of the hard-boiled thriller, a genre in which I had immersed myself over the previous ten years. And the excitement of reading a thriller was not dissimilar to the excitement of doing a crossword puzzle. But American crosswords didn't do it for me. The *New York Times*, which has the best-known American puzzle, seemed to lack the narrative quality of the British puzzles. Its clues were too literal, its meanings too obvious. They lacked also a common vocabulary, the difference between cricket, perhaps, and baseball.

Only cricket could have provided a clue as ambiguous as this in *Private Eye:* "Fanny needs to be probed for this libel on the game of cricket (5,4)."* Sometimes, however, this literal quality creates narratives of its own.

In January 1998, for example, the *Times* crossword editor, Will Shortz, allowed a young man to propose to his girlfriend by putting a message into the *New York Times* crossword. By his own admission Shortz was a little suspicious when Bill Gottlieb called him. "Well, at first," Shortz told me, "I thought I couldn't do this. I couldn't let the *Times* be used for something so personal. But then I called him up, and he seemed to me to be an earnest and sincere young man, and completely in love with Emily. And so I agreed."

"So anyway," Gottlieb told me, "Emily's doing the puzzle and I'm reading the rest of the paper and pretending not to know anything, and watching as she becomes suspicious. She fills in her name, and then my name. And then one answer is 'Will you marry me?' and she gets that. And then we had 'yes' as an answer. And the clue for 'yes' was "Hoped-for answer to 'Will you marry me?'"

"And by then," Bill continued, "she knew something was up, and that's when I asked her, properly, to marry me."

"And I said, 'Yes,'" says Emily.

.   .   .

*SMEAR TEST, where smear = libel and test = game of cricket. Cyclops, who sets the puzzles in *Private Eye*, says this clue created "howls of protest."

My girlfriend and I are more or less in love. We have returned home to London to the places and the work we know and trust. We have enrolled our children in school and unpacked the attic.

Each morning the *Guardian* is delivered through the door of our house.

Its thud, as it lands on the carpet, reminds me of the time the police came calling.

CUT TO:

The hallway of a terraced house in north London. It is five A.M. *There is a loud banging on the door. A pregnant woman staggers downstairs and opens the door. There are four men there. Two are wearing suits, and two are in the uniforms of the metropolitan police.*

OFFICER: We're looking for Mr. Balfour.

After years as an activist in South Africa, my girlfriend has a deeply ingrained distrust of policemen, especially those who call in the early hours of the morning.

CUT TO:

The pregnant woman's face hardens.

WOMAN: Who? What is this? What time is it?

OFFICER: Mr. Balfour. *(He consults a piece of paper.)* This is his house, isn't it?

WOMAN: No.

OFFICER: No?

WOMAN: No.

OFFICER: He doesn't live here?

WOMAN: No.

I am a good sleeper, in the sense that I sleep deeply and wake refreshed. On being woken by the noise downstairs I got up to see what was happening. My feet appeared at the top of the stairs at precisely the moment my girlfriend was denying me for the third time.

OFFICER: Mr. Balfour?

MAN *(brightly)*: That's me. How can I help?

The police officer looks at the woman.

WOMAN: Fuck. *(She pauses.)* I need some coffee.

The officers take us through to our kitchen. They crowd me. One holds me up against a wall with his hand to my throat. They tell my girlfriend to forget the coffee, and not to move. I have a sense I am about to get it, though I am not sure exactly what "it" will be. One of the men looks particularly restless. He looks like he would like to hit something. He has a flat stare that suggests I will do nicely. From time to time he goes out to the front door, to check that the street is quiet. Each time he returns, my interrogator looks at him, and he nods briefly.

There will be no witnesses.

They start asking about an old car my girlfriend and I used to own. One day it packed up and was not worth repairing. Some months before the police came calling, I paid a man to tow it away. But now the police want to know everything about it, and I cannot help them. I do not know the name of the man who towed it away. I cannot remember what he looked like. I didn't notice his tow truck. I can't say when, exactly, it was. Yes, I regret not having transferred the car to his name. I now own a new Citroën. Yes, it is the one parked outside. No, I bear the British state no ill will. No, I have no Irish connections.

Irish connections?

The questioning takes some time. For perhaps two hours they ask the same questions over and over. Since we are being cooperative they do not handcuff us, but I remember being very afraid. I remember the extraordinary level of understated aggression that the four men brought to their task. I remember longing for a cup of tea.

Eventually they believe me. They are sorry to have disturbed us, but they are sure we will understand. The car, still registered in my name, has been found stuffed with explosives. While one of them goes out to his vehicle, presumably to run some more checks on my girlfriend and me, we have "that cup of coffee." One of the men not in uniform notices the previous day's *Guardian*, with, perhaps, two clues complete.

"I prefer the *Times* myself," he says. "The *Guardian* is always trying to be too clever by half."

I am not sure that this is true, although the ability to do crosswords is assumed to be some sort of measure of intelligence.

Bletchley Park, the British code-breaking center in the Second World War, used a crossword puzzle as part of a test for potential code breakers. By today's standards it is ridiculously simple, a halfway house between concise and cryptic crosswords. It included clues like "The War (anag) 6" for "wreath," which hardly stretches the mind.

There is, nevertheless, no doubt that all the broadsheet setters are trying to be clever, although they may differ in their estimation of the solvers. Otherwise, what's the point? But they are trying also to please, and a setter can only do this if he has a real sense of the level of skill that his solvers will bring to the party. There is not much point in being too clever.

For the better setters the ideal is not to be clever, but to be surprising. The intention is to stimulate, not to test.

Adrian Bell, in his introduction to an anthology of crosswords brought out to mark the fiftieth anniversary of the *Times* puzzle, wrote this: "Yet a strictness of definition of the word sought must be included in the clue as an essential part of it. The complexity of association was encouraged." Every clue, he goes on to say, must tell a story which is "exact and rigorously grammatical, while the wording, whatever it said, said also something entirely different."[15]

This was in 1980, and Adrian Bell had set the first puzzle, which appeared in the *Times* on February 1, 1930, and the anniversary puzzle, which appeared in the *Times* on February 1, 1980. His key assertion is that "complexity of association was encouraged," and the calculation is to decide just how complex it can be.

Bell was a farmer and claimed that "the ideal occupation for dreaming up clues was harrowing ten acres of clods behind a horse that stumbles and plods." Many setters say the same sort of thing. Azed, who sets the fiendishly difficult puzzle in the *Observer*, claims to have his "big ideas" while walking the dog.

In Bell's case, it is not a great leap of the imagination to picture a lean and weathered man steering his plow between the sods of Norfolk earth. Nor is it hard to imagine how he came to describe what it is, exactly, that goes on in a crossword setter's mind:

"The setter's mind is more like a cinema than a reservoir. It is a sort of continuous performance of surrealist (though rigorously pertinent) imagery, related only by the interlockings and juxtapositions of orthography." It was only much later that I realized that this is true of the habitual solver too.

Crosswords free up the surrealist in us all.

Many years later, Adrian Bell's daughter told me that her father always said the point was not to make the solver chuckle. The point was to make him groan, "preferably with satisfaction."

He would test clues out on the kids at breakfast. "Die of cold? (3,4)"* came to her mind as we spoke.

It is early summer 1996, and I am in the town of Wellington, in Texas. A friend of mine and her husband and I have come to witness a rodeo. Later we find ourselves at the town dance.

*ICE CUBE.

The hot day has given way to a perfect evening. The dance is taking place at the tennis courts on the outskirts of town. There is a band, and wood smoke, and the smell of cooking meat. There are whoops and laughter, and the clink of beer bottles held in one hand. We approach cautiously, perhaps because my friend is from Vermont and her husband from Minnesota. They have come only recently to live in Texas.

There is a joke people tell in Vermont about the time the farmer from Texas came to visit. On seeing how small everything is in Vermont, the farmer from Texas is moved to remark, "Hell, where I come from it takes me all day just to drive across my land." To which the Vermonter replies, "Yes. I had a car like that once."

My friends and I stand out at the dance.

In particular I stand out. My friend and her husband look funny but have accents reminiscent of the local twang. I also look funny but have an accent that is way off the scale. I have neither cowboy boots nor a large hat, and my shirt is not checked.

Despite this we are adopted by Darrel. Darrel is on his own for the evening, in the sense that his wife is due to give birth to their child any moment now and is not, therefore, at the dance.

"Hell," says Darrel, "she's right fit to drop."

Darrel has everything a good Texan should have. He has a bushy moustache, cowboy boots, a ten-gallon hat, and a small air-conditioning business across the state line in Oklahoma. He also has two sons, a pregnant wife, and an abiding interest in England.

Darrel and I get on well.

My friend and her husband go off to dance. There is a band, and they and all the other couples on the tennis court are doing a kind of cloying shimmy which, I am told, is the Texas two-step.

Darrel is perhaps forty-five. Darrel's elder son is twelve, and named Matthew. Darrel himself looks as if he would like to dance, but would not wish it to be said that he was dancing when his wife went into labor.

Instead, we talk about baseball.

"It's like your cricket," Darrel says, "only fun."

We talk about cricket, which I maintain is fun, unlike (his) baseball.

I describe for him the rules of cricket. I have done this before and I know it is possible to do without getting into the confusion so beloved of gag writers.

But he does not understand when I explain to him that in cricket, when a batsman (batter) gets ready to face the bowler (pitcher), the side of the field (left field, if he is a right-handed player) facing his backside is called the "on" side. And the other side (right field) is called the "off" side.

"Why?" he asks.

"Because," I reply, and he has to make do with that.

Many years later I have a conversation with a man who runs a crossword website from Newcastle upon Tyne. Many of those who join the site come from the United States. They join looking for those elusive English puzzles, the same puzzles that are not printed in the local paper in Pittsburgh or Tallahassee. This man tells me that he gets a constant stream of inquiries about clues from American subscribers. "Usually," he says, "they want to know why 'leg' means 'on.'"

"Leg" means "on" to those who play cricket.

I am one of those who play cricket.

Back in Wellington, Texas, in the warm summer of 1996, Darrel and I talk about the Royal Family. For Darrel, in common with most Americans, there is only one Royal Family. Darrel has no interest in European royalty, and almost certainly no knowledge of African or Asian royalty. He uses the term "European" pejoratively.

He is slightly disappointed that I have not met Diana.

He does not understand the Queen's hats.

He thinks Charles should be "run out of town with a cattle prod."

I find it increasingly hard to disagree with Darrel.

We clink our glasses and let a companionable silence descend on us as we watch the dancing couples. The current number is winding its weary way to its end.

Darrel takes a deep breath.

A proper hero would have read that deep breath correctly.

.   .   .

He takes a swig of beer, and turns to me.

"Hell," he says, "would ya like to dance?"

I jump half out of my shoes.

Try anything once, I say to myself, except suicide and incest.

"Sure," I said. "Why not? Thank you. I'd love to dance."

Darryl happily misreads my misreading.

He puts his fingers to his lips and gives a piercing whistle, the sort of whistle that could summon a herd of cattle from halfway across Texas, or all the way across Vermont.

"Matthew," he says. "MATTHEW! Go find a woman. My friend here wants to dance!" And moments later Matthew returns with Judith, who takes my hand and teaches me the Texas two-step. The Texas two-step is not unlike a crossword clue, in that the solvers and the setters are treading different paths, albeit to the same end.

Darrel meant what he said. He only wanted to know whether I wanted to dance. He was not asking me to dance with him.

This, I decided, is the problem with American crosswords.

In England they put it like this. You should say what you mean, but you need not mean what you say. In America, however, you must say what you mean and mean what you say.

Years later I entered the American Crossword Tournament, and I discovered that this is not necessarily the case. American crosswords need neither say what they mean nor mean what they say. They have a different purpose, which is to make it possible for the solver to get the answer without ever knowing if it is the right one. Will Shortz, of the *New York Times*, tells the story of a puzzle set by Jeremiah Farrell that appeared in the paper in November 1996 on the day of the presidential election in which Bill Clinton and Bob Dole were the leading candidates. American puzzles do not do you the courtesy of telling you how many letters are in each answer, and this is the key, because there were, deliberately, two possible solutions to the puzzle.

The defining clue was for 39 and 43 across: "Lead Story in tomorrow's newspaper!," which corresponded to two seven-letter spaces. We have, at this stage, no way of knowing whether it is a word or words, whether it is a phrase of part of a phrase. And we certainly do not know that there are two possible answers.

So we look at the checking letters. Thirty-nine down was clued as "Black Halloween animal," for a three-letter space. In Britain this would cause howls of protest because, clearly, it can be a "cat" or a "bat." There is nothing to tell us which, and since the only letter that differs is the B or C of 39 across, we have to solve that to know.

And so it went on. Forty down could have been "oui" or "lui." Forty-one could have been "ira" or "bra." And so on. For each checked letter in the answer there were two possible answers. It is only when we get the two possible answers to 39 and 43 across that we see that the ambiguity is deliberate. For the answer— depending on the result of the election—could have been either "Clinton Elected" or "Bob Dole Elected," either of which could have been the "lead story in tomorrow's newspaper." If the setter had given the number of letters—(7,7) or (3,4,7)—it would have been a giveaway.

Not surprisingly, many people got the answer wrong (they should have looked at the polls!) and wrote in to complain. Technically it is a beautiful puzzle, and it delivers a substantial payoff. But for the solver there is the possibility of enormous frustration. Bill Clinton himself, presumably because he won the election, is said to have thought it "wonderful" and to have gone around showing it to his aides in preference to working on the details of his second inaugural address.

In Britain we do things differently. Remember the clue: "Linguist and Philosopher opposed to Vietnam War writing in prison (7)"? Let's consider the technicalities.

We know by now that the trick is to decide what it means. Then decide what type of clue it is. Then solve the damn thing, and move on.

But this is not how I experience crosswords. What happens with me is that I get the first and second steps correct. I decide what it means. I solve it. But do I move on? The hell I do. What I do is look for the story, and the story is not that of the setter. The story comes from me.

The clue is the trigger.

My memories are the bullet.

Who knows where they will go?

.   .   .

So what does the clue mean? It is tempting to accuse Pasquale, the setter, of being too clever by half. Clearly the definition is more than one word, because we are only looking for a seven-letter answer. And the definition in this case is deliberately long and misleading. The definition is "Linguist and Philosopher opposed to Vietnam War." And this is misleading because words like "opposed to" usually crop up in clues in other senses. They mean one constituent part of the answer next to another, or they indicate a reversal. But in this clue they are meant literally. The answer is a Linguist and a Philosopher known to have opposed the Vietnam War.

Once we know the definition, the rest is easy. There is only one candidate: Noam Chomsky, professor of linguistics at the Massachusetts Institute of Technology, and the answer is "Chomsky."

But why?

Well (deep breath) because MS = manuscript = "writing" is in "choky" = prison. Or at least choky = prison in Britain. In South Africa we would say "chookie" (or, more probably, *tjoekie*). But I have been in England a long time now, and I am happy to acknowledge the legitimacy of "choky."

And the clue does what a clue should do. It means what it says. The definition is accurate and specific. The constituent parts are precise and legitimate. There is no extraneous material. Although the definition is long, it is deliberately long, so as to send the solver off on a tangent. And the solver will not mind, because it is an interesting tangent, as tangents should be.

anyone,
anytime,
anywhere

In 1996, under a sky lit by starlight and an old moon, Matthew, the son of my new friend Darrel, procured (if that's the word) Judith, who wheeled me about until I was sufficiently skilled at the Texas two-step. And then we changed hands and it was my turn to lead.

You could say the same of crosswords. They started in America, but the British have long since become sufficiently skilled, and have started to lead.

Crossword puzzles have become a part of daily life in Britain. Every day millions of people attempt the cryptic crosswords in the broadsheet papers, and many more attempt the simple or "quick" crosswords.

It wasn't always this way.

There are some dissenting voices, but the general consensus is that crosswords began in New York in 1913 when an English émigré, Arthur Wynne, produced a puzzle, which was then published in the New York *World*. Wynne was the editor of the "Fun" section of the newspaper, and he put in the crossword only because he was having trouble filling his space quota. He in fact called it a "Word Cross," and he gave the readers the simplest of simple guides to how to solve it: "Fill in the small squares with words which agree with the following definitions." Wynne was always very modest in describing his role in creating what has for almost a century been America's favorite indoor pastime. "All I did," he said, "was take an idea as old as language and modernize it by the introduction of the black squares."

Wynne, who had in fact come to the United States from Liverpool, continued to set crosswords for some years after that, but the form really took off in the 1920s, when two recent graduates in New York set out to make their fortune in publishing. Their names were Simon and Schuster, and their first book was called the *Cross Word Puzzle Book*. Crosswords were an immediate hit, and soon were a part of daily life. So much so, in fact, that, when the U.S. Postal Service issued sets of stamps to commemorate each decade of the twentieth century, they included in the collection for the 1910s a stamp with Arthur Wynne's pioneering first crossword. Another commemorative stamp showed that other British immigrant success, Charlie Chaplin, and another—of course—the First World War. But it is a measure of the popularity of the crossword that it came to represent an entire decade. At least, it did in the United States.

At the time the English were not amused. In 1924, from its loftiest heights, the *Times* declared that "All America has succumbed to the crossword puzzle," which it claimed was "a menace because it is making devastating inroads on the working hours of every rank and society." By way of corroboration, the New York correspondent of the *Times* estimated in 1924 that Americans spent five million hours every day doing crossword puzzles, and that many of these hours should in fact have been working hours.

The *Times* was horrified, but the paper, not for the last time, was behind the times. While it is hard to fault the logic, it was surely not hard to imagine that Britain was a society just crying out for something to do in its leisure time. Which—let's face it—is often spent indoors.

In the 1920s Queen Mary and future Prime Minister Stanley Baldwin were early converts to crosswords, as were millions of newspaper readers. Within five years of Simon and Schuster's groundbreaking book, every British paper carried a crossword every day. And over the past seventy years, it is the British papers that have expanded and developed crosswords, and turned them into the cryptic and sometimes comic masterpieces we have come to expect. Quite how this happened no one knows. Various attempts have been made to trace the process, however. Adrian Bell, who started it, puts a substantial amount of responsibility at the door of Ronald Carton, his first puzzle editor at the *Times*. "Curious without the animals (3)" had, for example, been permissible in the American papers. But it was instantly taboo at the *Times*, where it was declared that a clue must have both the actual definition *and* the constituent parts or cryptic definition. Although "Curious without the animals (3)" is a perfectly adequate way of generating I.O.U. (take "curs" = animals out of "curious"), it is not an acceptable clue because it does not give a definition. "That clue," Bell wrote, "would not have passed muster with Ronnie, because it contained no indication of what the subtraction *meant*. That must be included as ambiguously as you liked, within dictionary sanction."

Dictionary sanction is an idea that preoccupies the more rule-bound setters. Don Manley, author of the Chambers *Crossword Manual*,[16] devotes several chapters to it. The question of definition comes out of the single most important premise that binds cryptic crossword setters together: The clue must be unambiguous. There can and should be only one possible answer to each clue. It comes into a notion of "fair play" that runs deeply through the British sense of what sport is for. In saying so, Manley is part of a tradition that now goes back some decades. An early chronicler of the "rules" of crosswords was A. F. Ritchie, who set puzzles in the *Observer* under the pseudonym of Afrit. In his 1949 book, *Armchair Crosswords*, Afrit wrote what has become the accepted basis for fairness and for the establishment of rules in British cryptic puzzles: "He may attempt to mislead by employing a form of words which can be taken in more than one way, and it is your fault if you take it the wrong way but it is his fault if you cannot logically take it the right way."[17]

This definition of fairness has been expanded over the years, particularly through the clue writing competitions of the *Observer*, run first by Afrit, then by Ximenes, and now by Azed. Ximenes published his *Art of the Crossword* in 1966,[18] and since then adherents of this particular school of crosswords call themselves "Ximenean." Rule-bound or not, it was people like Afrit and Ximenes who took these crosswords and changed them from an American pastime to a peculiarly British cultural form. It was Shed, who sets for the *Guardian* and the *Financial Times*, who told me, perceptively I thought, that Ximenes, like Marx, suffers from the quality of his disciples.

It is high summer 1999, and my son and I are in deepest Pennsylvania. At the U.S. Armed Forces International Air Show, held at the airport of the towns of Scranton and Wilkes-Barre, I am witnessing disciples of a different kind. We have come here with my girlfriend's father to see the U.S. military put on an extraordinary display of their past and present might. There is much to see. For my son the highlight is a jet-propelled truck that screams down the runway at an unlikely speed.

I am less easily pleased. I find the huge milling crowd disturbing. I find the combination of aviation fuel and barbecue smoke nauseating. I find the glare from the tarmac irritating. In anticipation of these feelings, my girlfriend has declined to join us. She and my daughters have preferred to remain by the lake, swimming and sunbathing.

I envy their decision, but I am also curious. I want to learn what brings all these people to this place. I am curious to experience an America hidden from the East Coast citadels I know better. Even in New York or Boston, people will remark that they "love my English accent," and I will smile politely (and smugly, since my "accent" remains stubbornly South African, or at least "not English"). But for all the stereotyping there is an assumption that I and the people of the East Coast media share values and experiences, and have read some of the same books. There is no such assumption in Scranton, Pennsylvania.

The announcer at the air show tells us that there are 80,000 people at the show, making it the biggest and best air show ever. He points us in the direction of the transport plane used during the Berlin airlift. He draws our attention to the Huey helicopter that saw service in Vietnam. He mentions the "fine concession stands" that surround the tarmac. He bids us enjoy the show.

And he tells us about the F-15 bomber that, at that moment, is going through its paces in the sky above us. Its huge gray wings cast their shadow on the crowd as the bomber hangs in the air.

"This," the announcer tells us, "is the F-15." It is, he goes on, a very fine aircraft. It has all you could ask of an aircraft. It has speed and power and range and versatility. What it is, he concludes, is "a shining example of America's ability to kill anyone, anytime, anywhere, under any circumstances."

He really said that. He said that this plane demonstrates America's ability to kill anyone.

Anywhere.

Anytime.

Under any circumstances.

This was in 1999, some years before the United States and Britain put this particular theory to the test. The remarks drew from the crowd a great shout of appreciation and ringing applause, which chimed neatly with the roar of the F-15's engines as the pilot pointed its nose to the heavens and disappeared into the sun.

Swamped by the noise and heat, I felt a disquiet at what I now realize was a relatively modest exhibition of American triumphal gloating. My response was to engage a colonel of the United States Air Force in conversation.

I told the colonel that I found the idea that he could kill me anywhere, anytime, and under any circumstances unsettling. I mentioned that as a foreigner I found this less comforting than perhaps did the massed ranks of Americans at the air show. I pointed out that those of us who have disagreements with the United States assert our right to disagree, and to assert our own view of the world.

He said I was the first person he had ever met to say these things.

I asked him if he had ever been abroad, to which he said no.

We agreed that this probably explained it.

And so we talked about baseball. In this respect I am a good traveler. I can discuss baseball with Americans in much the same way as I can discuss *kabadi* with the citizens of Bangalore or cricket with Australians. I defer to their expertise, but I have my own view.

At some point in the conversation the colonel mentioned a particular game of baseball. It is a game he umpired, and it took place in Sarajevo, in Bosnia.

"But," I objected, "you said you had never been abroad."

"Hell no," he agreed, and then seeing my look of doubt he went on to explain. "By the time I got there," he said, "it was ours."

I feel the same way about cryptic crosswords.

By the time I made Britain my home, they were ours. Americans still have their own form of crosswords, best exemplified in the *New York Times*, and indeed run their own cryptic puzzles in publications like the *Nation* and *Atlantic Monthly*. But it seems to me that, as an art form, the cryptic puzzle has been appropriated by the British. We have made them our own, and have written the rules in our own image.

That the British had written the rules in their own image, and that this image, when I looked at it, seemed to me to fit me well, is at the heart of this story. I found that what appealed to me was not only the general idea of British crosswords, but the particular form they take in British broadsheets, and in the *Guardian* in particular.

I am not, for example, a *Telegraph* person (although I buy it on Mondays for the sports coverage, especially during the cricket season and after weekends on which there have been Six Nations rugby fixtures).

I do like, though, the story of how the longtime editor of the *Telegraph* crossword got into trouble for this clue: "Outcry at Tory assassination (4,6)." The answer is BLUE MURDER. It is not, on the face of it, an objectionable clue. But it appeared in the *Telegraph* on July 30, 1990, the day that Ian Gow, a junior minister in Margaret Thatcher's government, was blown up in the driveway of his home by the Provisional IRA. Under the circumstances it is not surprising that some people took offense, although the editor's defense—that the clue had been prepared weeks before, and that she had no foreknowledge of it—is not unreasonable.

How much greater, one wonders, would have been the offense, had the clue been phrased as it appeared in the *Guardian* recently. "Clamor for Tory assassination (4,6)"[19] has a much more sinister edge, and it leaves one in no doubt as to the political sympathies of the setter and his presumed readership. Actually, that should be "their" readership. Gemini, the setter, is not one person, but two people.

All setters will tell you, however, that you cannot be too careful, nor can you presume too much. Everything you write is monitored by thousands. There is no knowing what will give offense. This is true in the United States too, only more so. The editor of the *New York Times* puzzle told me that 27 percent of Americans—more than 50 million people—occasionally do puzzles, a staggering number. The editor estimates that, through syndication and so on, perhaps five million people do each of the puzzles he edits.

Each newspaper has its own style. Some, like the London *Times*, do so very self-consciously. Others, most notably the *Guardian*, allow its setters a very free hand. The *Times* editors, particularly Brian Greer, but also John Grant and Mike Laws, have been known to issue memos to their stable of setters, setting out the requirements for the *Times* puzzles. John Grant, who at the age of seventy-seven still sets for the *Times*, gave me an insight into their differing editorial styles when I went to see him. Brian Greer, he said "was meddlesome. If he didn't like a clue it generally meant he could see a way of doing it better. But Mike Laws will either accept or reject a clue. If he doesn't like it, it is up to the setter to try again." By his own admission, John Grant was "somewhere between the two."

All compilers need a reason to begin a puzzle in a particular way. For some, it starts with a single word. Others prefer to have a bigger idea. And some—usually the professionals—just get on with it. One told me that he likes to have a theme because this gives him a reason to fill in the grid. Without the grid there will be no reason for one word to follow another. Another has a more prosaic view. "I don't do themes," he says. "Why would I? They don't pay extra." And a third told me this: "If you're going to fill in the grid, for heaven's sake start in the middle and work outward. If you start at the top left, the bottom right will be a real mess. Oh, and one other thing. Use words that you're going to be able to clue."

This seems to me to be good advice.

The words of another setter still lurk restlessly in the back of my mind. Most puzzles in a 15 x 15 grid will have somewhere between thirty and fifty words. "By the time you've put in seven words," she said, "they control the puzzle. They pretty much dictate what else is going to be in a puzzle. So choose your first words with care."

You could say the same of memoirs.

charades

It is the autumn of 1988. My girlfriend and I meet up in Minot, North Dakota. She has flown in from New York, I from London. We arrive on the same flight as a series of delegates to a Viking convention. My girlfriend has Viking blood (oh, all right, *Norwegian* blood) and looks (despite not being faux) not dissimilar to the serried ranks of faux-blond women in faux-Viking dress waiting to greet a series of surprisingly large men wearing helmets with horns sticking out of them.

We head north, into Canada, where we spend some time with friends. Our friends live in a homestead a little way outside of a town in southern Saskatchewan. He is a doctor; she is an artist. It is not a big town. We could walk two hundred yards and be a little way out of town. The friends are also South African. Like us they are interested to speculate on who it is they will become. Just as it seems impossible to us that we will one day be British, it seems unlikely to them that they will one day be Canadian.

But here they are. They buy Cheerios and drive big cars—or "units"—acquired from Ron's lot downtown. Downtown, in this case, means two stores past the post office.

Our friends lend us their car, and my girlfriend and I set off to drive across Canada. We are heading west, and this is, as it were, an innocent time before crosswords, and before children. At this point in my life no pretty girls have rebelled. The Indian summer evenings settle gracefully on the wheatfields. Oilrig derricks move in their rhythmic way against a golden harvest landscape. We move slowly but steadily along roads without corners. We pass towns called Forget and Arcola. We stop to look at the Olympic ski ramp in Calgary. In Banff I buy socks from the Hudson's Bay Company. The Hudson's Bay Company was something I remembered from books read as a child, books about huskies and polar bears, and men with chiseled jaws and flinty eyes who shot wolves and who sleep by firelight. It had not previously occurred to me that the Hudson's Bay Company was real.

As we drive across Canada, my girlfriend and I play memory games. We are trying to construct, from fragments, a plausible story of how, for example, we came to be sitting in a canoe on Lake Louise at just the moment the first blizzard of the winter came swirling in off the mountains.

"It all started," my girlfriend says, "when I was born."

"No, no," I argue, "it goes back much further than that."

It seems equally unlikely that we should, in the Rockies, be spending an evening with hunters out for the first day of the season. They wear plaid jackets and orange hats, and talk knowingly of ballistics. They find it as unlikely as we do that we should be there at all.

"Let me get this straight," says one, "you're driving across Canada for fun?"

"Uh-huh."

"Why?"

"Why are you hunting?" I ask.

"It's what men do," he says.

I am tempted to say, "There's your answer."

Instead my girlfriend and I play charades. She is very good at charades. As with crosswords, she has an instinct for the answer, and she can act. This puts her way ahead of me.

Charades is a key skill for solving crosswords. Many clues will be of the form "car" plus "nation" = "flower." The clue will disguise this a little. For example, it may be of the form "bloomer puts transport before country (9)," where "puts" is what is known as a "link word" to indicate the relationship between the synonym for the answer and the constituent parts.

The crossword setter can then make this more and more complicated. "Pretty girl in crimson rose (8)" is a charade clue, but instead of the constituent parts being in sequence, we have one ("belle") put "in" the other ("red") to give the answer ("re-belled").

From here it is a quick step to doing it backward or to disguise it in various ways (partial words, subtractive clues) and so on. Take, for example, "Tony transfigured and translated? Wait for it! (3,3)" The clue combines an anagram indicated by "transfigured" (which also serves as a wry comment on the pretensions of the British prime minister) and a translation of "and," and means "wait for it."

The process for the setters in working out the charade is first to break the word down into its constituent parts. Some words lend themselves more easily to this than others. "Hero," for example, does not immediately present a setter with too many possibilities, even if we accept that O can be "love." But if we accept that O is "love," the hero can be read as "her love," which suddenly has a whole host of other possibilities.

Or at least it does in a love story.

This is, of course, a love story.

In the chill of a Rocky Mountain night my girlfriend and I play charades. I realize now that the game was part of a process of developing an understanding with each other. At first each phrase takes a long time to work out. We try to do them elaborately. We try to do them bit by bit—first word, second word, and so on. There is frustration and laughter.

"Can't you see I'm doing a cakewalk?" asks my girlfriend. I had thought she was Jemima Puddleduck.

But as we put in the time, as we learn from our mistakes and from our successes, the codes become shorter and shorter. The body of assumed knowledge grows larger. We get to the answers more quickly. We develop the right to take short cuts.

This is what has happened with crosswords.

Crosswords use codes. Dictionaries supply lists of abbreviations, symbols, numbers, and other bits and pieces that crop up regularly in clues. Roman numerals, for example, are legitimate, and are frequently used to indicate individual letters. V can mean five, or D five hundred. *"Model"* may mean T, as in Model T Ford. *"Apprentice"* may mean L as in Learner Driver (in Britain, learner drivers have to have a large red L on their vehicles). *"Volunteer"* may mean TA as in the Territorial Army. "Writer" in a crossword puzzle will frequently mean "pen," or even a kind of pen, just as "flower" can mean a river as well as a bloom.

And so on. Some areas of life are richer than others. Cricket delivers to setters and solvers a wealth of expressions and phrases. LBW, for example. Or just R for river, so that we can have a clue like "It's very exciting when the stream enters the river (8)" in which river stands for R.

Many years later I am in Toronto in connection with a television project. The project is one of the most complex we have attempted, at least in respect to the number of people involved and the sources of finance represented. People in the movie industry describe the process of getting together the financing for a movie as the process of standing in the middle of a large room with, say, twelve doors. The art of producing, then, is the art of closing all twelve doors at once while remaining in the middle of the room. It is what you might call a process of orchestration.

Don Manley writes the same way of the process of compiling crosswords. Every possibility has a set of subsidiary possibilities, and part of the art of the setter is to engage properly in the orchestration of these many small parts. The orchestration happens at many levels, and the rhythm and the harmonies matter as much as the melody itself. "Here is Grub Street. Writer's about (6)," for example, has many deceptions. The first is that the grammar has been used to deceive the solver as to the meaning of the answer. The meaning is in fact "Here is grub," meaning a place when food might be found. But because the grammar unites "grub" with "street," and because Grub Street is a well-known epithet for "the journalistic trade" in Britain, it is very hard to get away from the assumptions we bring to bear. But once we have worked out that we are looking for the name of a place where food might be found, it is relatively easy to take a word for "writer" and put it around ST for "street."

I am in a bistro in Toronto, watching the traffic on Bloor Street. With me is a fellow producer. Ours, at this moment, is not a happy lot. The many doors we are supposed to be closing are wide open, and a chill wind blows through them.

We do what anyone would have done. We order more coffee and have a go at the crossword in the Toronto *Globe and Mail*.

It is a very easy puzzle.

But even within easy puzzles there are stories waiting to be told. The stories may come from the setter, or they may come from the solvers.

My producing colleague, after a long e-mail correspondence on the subject of the sort of men who do crosswords, and their likely—or unlikely—merits in other fields has included a number of her colleagues in the debate. One writes to me as follows: "Although I keep well away from sad men with roll-ups, as a crossword aficionado I have a favorite clue. It appeared about five years ago in the Cryptic Crossword [which relies heavily on anagrams] of the Toronto *Globe and Mail* on [note this well] November the 11th. The clue was 'Country which makes me angry (7).' Toronto members of the trans-Rhine community re-acted, well, angrily."

The phrase "the trans-Rhine community" appeals to me. In the great supermarket of identities, my correspondent is refer-ring to people who choose to remain "trans-Rhine" in an even more remote sense than that by which I might claim to be South African. And from that they had extrapolated a sense of grievance that unspoken rules had been transgressed.

Let me take you back to 1993. I am producing a documentary film about work. The film stars and is directed by a Cumbrian poet of some repute. He comes from the immediate postwar generation and has lived through Britain's late-Imperial decline and its consequent search for a different identity. His roots are deep in the mining and shipping industries of Tyneside, but even in his teens, he said, he was questioning why men of his father's generation "bothered to work at all."

At the age of fourteen he was given a union card and sent off to the shipyards. As it happened, he chose not to work in the shipyards. He chose instead to become a poet, even though the shipyards purported to offer a job for life.

At first glance this does not seem a good decision. Poetry offered a lifetime of poverty. At second glance it looks like genius.

In retrospect it turns out that being a poet is a job for life, whereas being a shipyard worker in Tyneside or Wearside is not. The poet, as it happens, has made the right decision.

The poet and I are to interview a minister in the government of John Major. The minister at the time belonged to the "wet" wing of the Conservative Party. Despite this he has managed to forge for himself a career of middling intensity.

The minister talks eloquently in the interview conducted in the pressroom in his department. He tells us how much he enjoys his position as minister. He tells us it gives him enormous pleasure to work in public service. He tells us he does not mind the "low pay." He would happily sacrifice the fortune to be made in the private sector in order to make a contribution to his country.

What the minister and his minders do not know is that we have recently been filming a man called Mick. Mick was a worker from the shipyards that have now closed. He has many skills.

Mick has recently told us how much he would love to work; that it is through work that he has discovered himself. It was his job, and his membership in the union, that gave him the identity he has worn for thirty years. But now Mick has no job.

He is putting a brave face on it.

He says that he has used the time to read. He has discovered poetry. He has learned the names of flowers. But it is written in his face, and in his eyes, and in the cracks around the edge of his voice, that what Mick wants more than anything in the world is a job.

He would, he says, be willing to take a job paying £1.80 an hour, if he could get the hours.

But he can't get the hours.

In the slightly overheated quiet of a room in Whitehall, the poet listens politely while the minister tells us how much he enjoys *his* job, how rewarding it is, and how much satisfaction it gives.

And then the poet asks him a question that changes the whole tone of the interview; one, in fact, that brings it to an abrupt and tense end.

"Would you," says the poet, "enjoy the job if you were paid one pound eighty per hour?"

"If you could get the hours," he adds, to fill the silence.

"No," said the minister when the microphones were turned off. "This is not what I agreed to."

You could say the same of Mick.

.   .   .

From time to time, crossword setters and solvers will meet and argue about the rules by which they are governed, about what it is that they have agreed to. There are those who argue that there are no rules, only understandings. There are those who argue that a constitution of sorts has grown up, rather like the British constitution. It is not codified, or if it is, it is in a wide selection of publications and "common law" which vary as to legitimacy and to the intention of the writers. Some, like Azed in the *Observer,* and Ximenes before him, have used a long-standing relationship with solvers to arrive at definitions of what is and is not legitimate. It is possible, for example, to subscribe to a publication in which Azed will provide a running commentary on clues and their legitimacy.

This practice was started by Ximenes. It is a measure of his influence that all setters I have spoken to started off by expressing a view as to whether or not they are "Ximenean." The phrase has come to mean those for whom attention to the detail of the rules is as important as attention to the spirit of the enterprise. Rufus, for example, not strictly a Ximenean, nevertheless said to me that he would not now allow himself to use a clue like "Émigré beaten up by the authorities (6)" on the grounds that the "by" is superfluous. Since it is of the essence in a Ximenean clue that every word should have a role to play, this would not fit within the rules. Rufus himself says of this particular clue "With another ten years experience since then, I may have been doubtful of using the word 'by' as not strictly accurate, cryptically speaking! I would probably have changed it

round to summat like 'The authorities have émigré beaten up.'"
This seems to me to be a small point. The greater elegance of
the former version overrides the rule-bound nature of the
second.

Similarly, the editors of all the papers establish their "rules"
by custom and practice as much as by papal edict. But, small
disagreements aside, it seems clear to me that the "rules" of
crosswords allow for plenty of room for maneuvering. As one
editor put it, the "rules" are "like a steering wheel that has plenty
of play. As long as you stay on the road, you can wobble about
as much as you like."

I am beginning to understand that there are those within
the crossword world who are rigorous in their adherence to the
rules, and there are those, particularly on the *Guardian,* who
wobble very freely indeed.

It seems to me that this question of rules, and our relationship to them, is one of the central questions for those of us seek-
ing to define a new or different identity. It is a key question, for
example, in trying to understand the nature of the relationship
between those who govern and those who are governed. All
immigrants need to assess more explicitly than natives the ex-
tent to which they accede to the customs and laws of their
adopted land. It is easier to fit in, if we are allowed plenty
of play.

James C. Scott concludes his stunningly original book on
the nature of knowledge and its relationship to our political institutions like this: "Finally, that most characteristic of human

institutions, language, is the best model: a structure of meaning and continuity that is never still and ever open to the improvisations of all its speakers."[20]

In all I have read, I have yet to find a better description of the point of crosswords.

a form
of closure

It is fashionable when talking about crosswords to talk about how long it takes to solve them. For me these discussions remained academic. Seven years after I started, I had still not managed to complete, unaided, a single broadsheet crossword puzzle.

The day that, finally, I did complete a puzzle sticks in my mind.

I have only a limited acquaintance with cows. Once, as a boy, I milked one, and there was another time when in the foothills of the Drakensberg in South Africa I watched one calving while the farmer cursed it roundly right up to but not including the moment the calf emerged wetly into the world. At this point the farmer smiled broadly and looked at the distant peaks.

"Nothing like it," he said, his voice breaking slightly. "Gets me every time."

Viewed from the comfort of a car or train window, cows add a comfortably ponderous presence to the passing scene. They do not, at first glance, appear to be dangerous or subversive. We are happy for them to be there. We are familiar with their outline and know, subliminally, that our and their well-being are connected. We do not often remark their presence, but we would notice their absence. They are part of the landscape of our lives.

You could say the same of crossword puzzles.

My apprenticeship in the art of crossword solving took place sporadically over a period of perhaps seven years. I graduated— if that's the word—at what the BBC calls 16.30 hours, Greenwich Mean Time, on the warm afternoon of March 1, 1997. I say "warm" because I was in South Africa at the time. At home, in Britain, it was still winter, and the football season.

Every afternoon during the winter months, the *BBC World Service* briefly loses its composure and takes a feed direct from the football-crazy contributors to *BBC Radio Five Live*. The switch occurs just after the four o'clock news, which, allowing for a news summary, means listeners to the World Service "join" the commentators just after the start of the second half of the games on that afternoon. From Mongolia to the Falklands, men of a certain age and inclination hunker down over their radios and listen to Alan Green, Jimmy Armfield, and the rest of the BBC's team of commentators describe the antics of some the world's highest-paid clowns.

By March 1997 I have become a man of a certain age and inclination, and so it is that on the Saturday in question I am hunkered down over my radio. In fact, I have it cradled on my lap and am listening to it over the noise of the car engine as I head north along the new N2 highway in South Africa's Kwazulu Natal province. From time to time I adjust the aerial, hoping in vain for clearer reception.

South Africa, during the winter months, is two hours ahead of Britain. This means that by the time I tune in to the World Service football, it is just after six, and already almost dark.

Dusk comes fast to northern Kwazulu Natal. Since I am heading north, the orange glow to my left is quickly swallowed by deep darkness. Since it is that time of month, I know that the Indian Ocean beyond the marshes, dunes, and plantations on my right will be soon flecked with the silver light of an early moon. And since this is northern Kwazulu Natal on a Saturday evening, the roads are full of moving vehicles, moving people, moving animals. I have picked up one hitchhiker, a student from the University of Zululand at Ulundi, and we speed past many others. They stand with their fingers raised for the taxis that ply this route. They look like sailors in search of a fair wind.

Then there are cane trucks and timber lorries to avoid. This is harvest time, and the cane trucks are particularly dangerous, spewing shards of cut cane onto the road.

My traveling companion is carrying a briefcase full of books, and wearing a blue shirt and a red tie. He is perhaps twenty-five years old, and is returning home after working at a shop in Richard's Bay. It is, he tells me, his habit to use the long hours spent waiting for a lift beside the road to study, which explains the briefcase full of books. We move on from a discussion about his course in business administration to talking about football.

The reach of football is global, and it turns out that he and I each have club allegiances in both Britain and South Africa, but his allegiances are diametrically opposed to mine. For nearly a decade I lived near the Arsenal football stadium in north London, and during that time I became not exactly a fan, but an interested fellow traveler. I can name most first-team players. I know what trophies they have won. I note the team's scores, and I track their position in the league tables. For some years their position has been second to the all-conquering Manchester United.

My companion, by contrast, is a Liverpool fan.

1997 is a trying time to be a Liverpool fan.

When in South Africa I pay lip service to the fortunes of another club, Orlando Pirates. Orlando Pirates are one of the oldest clubs from Soweto. The founders, from the Orlando section of Soweto, chose the name Pirates after watching an Errol Flynn movie in 1937. I know this because I once produced a documentary film about the club in which they were described variously as "the people's team" and "the Liverpool of South

Africa." While making the film, I attended some games. I spent one memorable afternoon at a game talking to man who wore a dead chicken fashioned as a hat. I spent another wondering unhappily what animal it was that provided the meat in the stew I had just purchased from a roadside vendor. I was confident that the animal had died of natural causes at a very old age. Orlando Pirates won both those games and, since everyone loves a winner, I quickly developed an affection for the team.

When I am in South Africa, therefore, I take an interest in how Pirates are doing. My companion, of course—since this is Kwazulu Natal—supports AmaZulu. He is delighted to hear that I once filmed a game at the so-called "Soccer City" stadium outside Soweto in which AmaZulu, the underdogs, beat Pirates, the overwhelming favorites, one-nil.

In the film, one of the Pirates fans says after the game, "We beat them from start to finish. The only thing was, we lost the game."

This is one of my favorite sayings. I have often felt this way about crosswords. The editor of the *Times* crossword once told me that "the setter is entering a game in which the point is to lose gracefully." In my experience the setters do not always lose, because at this point I have yet to complete a puzzle.

This is weighing on my mind, and even as we listen to the football, I am working away at a crossword clue that has been bugging me for some weeks. The clue comes from a puzzle in a South African paper, but the puzzle has been lifted from the *Guardian* in Britain.

The clue is this: "XI ay 100 (7)."

It is the final clue in the puzzle. I have filled in all the rest, and so I even know the checked letters. And I have only this one clue to go. This is as close as I have ever gotten to finishing a *Guardian* puzzle. This is as close as I have gotten to finishing any cryptic puzzle. I am a single clue away from ending my seven-year apprenticeship in the art of crossword solving.

And I cannot, for the life of me, get it.

XI ay 100.

Blank . . . V . . . blank . . . R . . . blank . . . O . . . blank.

Seven letters.

I cannot even work out where to begin. The reason is that I have forgotten the key discipline required by crossword solvers, which is this: Ignore the surface meaning and ask yourself one question, "Does the answer mean or describe the first or the last word or phrase of the clue?"

Well, which is it? A synonym for eleven, or a synonym for one hundred? Though even if I had had the discipline to ask myself the question, how the hell would I have known? And anyway, what surface meaning?

This is a very difficult clue.

My companion knows nothing of crosswords, and I do not trouble him with this particular problem. Instead we listen again to the football in England. On this particular day, Arsenal are away to Everton.

By the time the World Service tunes in, the game is already beyond doubt. Bergkamp and Wright have given Arsenal a two-nil lead in the first half, and they never look in danger of losing it. My companion is more interested in the names. "Why 'Arsenal'?" he wants to know, and I explain how the club started off as the team of the workers at the Woolwich Arsenal. It was only after the team's great triumphs in the 1930s that my particular part of north London was renamed in the club's honor.

I explain that I live only two hundred meters from the Arsenal football ground. My companion is impressed.

"*Hai*," he says, and he sucks his teeth, to show he is impressed.

"And Everton," he says, "where does that name come from?"

As it happens, I know this too. I have not been there, but I know that the club is somewhere on Merseyside, and that commentators talk from time to time about "the blue half of the city" to distinguish Everton fans from those of the more illustrious Liverpool Football Club, who wear red. I know also that the name was adopted in 1879 from the road near the park where the club once played. Prior to that they were known by their nickname, the Mighty Moonlighters. Everton Road on Merseyside was also home to Ye Ancient Everton Toffee House, which is how the club came to get their new nickname, the Toffees. This is the sort of thing you know, if you have spent enough time in Britain.

It occurs to me now that I have spent enough time in Britain.

But at the time, I was driving too fast through the dark of a Kwazulu night, and I neither thought this, nor cared.

Because suddenly I have it.

I had it!

Everton!

The answer was "Everton"—a team, which is to say an "XI"*—made up of "ever" which can mean "ay," as in "ever and ay" and "ton," which, in cricket, is a score of one hundred (or more).

"Got it," I yelled, much to my companion's surprise, "I've got it. It's 'Everton'!"

I punched the air with my fist and grinned triumphantly at my bemused companion.

"Arsenal are winning?" he said.

"I'm talking about a clue," I said, which served only to increase his confusion.

"Clue?" he said, not having one himself.†

Which is when the cow strolls in front of us.

I close my eyes.

There is a squealing of tires, followed by a low moan, which may have been the cow and may have been me. I think it would not be fair to say I hit the cow, because the cow eventually walks off unhurt. But in a sequence of events the details of which remain obscure to me, the cow somehow comes to be sitting on the bonnet of my car, gently lowing. And my companion and I come to be staring at each other with wild eyes, aware that we have each narrowly missed an untimely death.

---

*"XI" means "team" because both football and cricket have eleven players to a team.
†"! (4,3,4,1,4)" is commonly used to give people the basic idea of crosswords, the answer being DOES NOT HAVE A CLUE.

I get out and inspect the car. There is nothing else wrong with it. Only the muddy hoof marks on the windshield suggest that a cow has been there. I later tell the people at the car rental place that I have no idea how the top of the bonnet of the car came to be dented. "Perhaps someone sat on it in a parking lot. You know what those kids are like," I suggest. "I never saw what happened," I add.

"Can I see your driver's license?" the woman asks.

I pull it out and hand it to her.

"I thought so," she says. "You're English, aren't you? I recognized your accent."

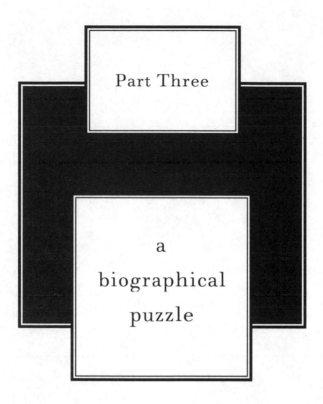

Part Three

a
biographical
puzzle

16

the
game

In retrospect it all seems obvious.

Crosswords are a game, and for the setter the point of the game is to lose gracefully. The point for the solver is to win, but the solver should do this gracefully as well. The solver who is impatient, who competes against the clock, is missing the point. Stories must find their own pace. There is no particular merit in a story that can be told quickly. The merit in a story is to do with the way character and plot combine.

The same is true of émigrés. Perhaps the phrase is "active acquiescence." I have been in Britain for nearly twenty years, and during that time I have steadily, and increasingly, acquiesced to its view of itself. Sometimes it amuses me and sometimes I find it irritating, but, like crosswords, it is more often the former than the latter. And "amuses" is insufficiently strong. Much about Britain delights me. I feel privileged to be part of the sprawling cacophony of London, its many voices and innumerable stories. London, like other great cities, is an immensely satisfying place to live

In the course of making a film about the Channel Tunnel, I once climbed Shakespeare Cliff, just outside Dover. It was dawn, and we had come especially to get the shot of the great white chalk face as the sun rose. But that particular morning there was a dark cloud over the southern tip of England. We waited and watched in frustration as the minutes ticked by, knowing we would have to come back another day to get the shot. Nevertheless, being a professional, the cameraman set up the camera and waited. And at the perfect moment, in the perfect way, the cloud cover broke, the sun shone through, and what had been the blank impenetrable face of the cliffs became a shining tapestry of shadow and light.

We got the shot.

Since it was crosswords that offered me a grip on the seemingly blank cliff face of Britain, I started teaching myself about them and the people who create and solve them. I was curious about how they worked, and I was curious to ask the question that had been bothering me since Chad. Can a crossword have a personality? Who are the setters?

Who is Rufus?

I meet Rufus for a drink in a pub in St. Martin's Lane in central London. He comes complete with notes and anecdotes and is very helpful to me. Later we correspond from time to time. He was born in Wolverhampton in 1932, and he left school at fifteen to join the Royal Navy, where he won his commission with the Fleet Air Arm. It was while in the service that he discovered a talent for entertaining. When he resigned, he became an Entertainment Officer, a "redcoat," at Butlins. For the past forty-odd years he has been making his living, and his name, as a comedy-magician, which is, he says, "as good a definition of a crossword compiler as any."

Rufus is famous in the crossword world for the sheer volume of his output. To date, he has had more than 57,000 puzzles published, and his average output is thirty-eight puzzles each week. His millionth clue appeared in the *Telegraph* in 1989. He tells how one *Telegraph* solver even used a puzzle he set to specify terms in her will. The will was contested, but the courts accepted its legitimacy and its peculiar form of expression.

Rufus is famous for keeping meticulous records of his clues. He has been cataloguing, first on cards and now on a computer, all his clues since 1963. I ask him about "émigré" (see Chapter 4), and he is able to look it up and tell me when and where it was published (*Guardian*, 1991). Similarly, I ask him about "Pretty girl in crimson rose (8)," and he is able to tell me that it is not one of his. "But I did use," he writes, "'Pretty girl in red and rose (8),' in the early 1980s, and 'Rose, a lovely girl in crimson (8)' in 1997. They all pretty much say the same thing." Some say that the quality of his clues suffer from volume fatigue. Others criticize his occasional reworking of the same clue—how could one not in a million clues?

Like other setters he has several other pseudonyms—Hodge in the *Independent,* and Dante in the *Financial Times*—but I know him as Rufus, just as I "knew" him a decade ago in Chad. He shows me a letter (subtitled "my favorite!") to the *Guardian* dating from March 1992. It reads "For me, Araucaria is the Beethoven of setters—immensely impressive, but labored and heavy-footed at times. Too many of his clues are tortuous and meaningless. The incomparable Rufus, on the other hand, is Mozart—concise, elegant, witty, sparkling . . ."

Like all professional entertainers, Rufus takes the business of self-promotion seriously. He gives me a list of favorites, some by himself, some by others, and then tells me one that is not on the list, which he credits to the author, Ian Polley.

"'Wrinkled old retainer,'" he says, "seven letters."

I think of Ben in the house in Nairobi.

I am some way off the mark.

"'Scrotum,'" says Rufus, with a chuckle.

I was learning about crosswords and crossword people. I was meeting the setters. I was also, I now realize, trying to pick from the firmament of possible identities one that I thought suited me.

I was trying to find the story that best fitted the facts.

Despite the diversions and the obstacles.

And notwithstanding my girlfriend. My girlfriend is of the view that my housework is suffering due to my interest in crosswords. I take the view that it is research for a book.

.   .   .

You will have noticed that most of my formative experiences have taken place outside of Britain, as have many of my formative crossword experiences. You will have noticed that since I settled in London I have been lucky enough to travel widely.

But I have always come back, each time a little bit different. Perhaps it runs in the family. Like all Balfours I have met, we claim to be related to Robert Louis Stevenson,[21] whose memoirs, published as *The Amateur Emigrant*, contain unnerving echoes of my own early attempts to be a man of the world. Entertainingly, Stevenson calls a large chunk of the book "Random Memories." Stevenson left Britain "for good" in 1888, and settled finally in Samoa, where he was buried after his death in 1894. In Samoa he acquired the name Tusitala, usually translated as "teller of tales," although I prefer "storyteller."

"Travel," he writes in *The Amateur Emigrant*, "is of two kinds. And this voyage of mine across the ocean combined both. . . . I was not only travelling out of my country in latitude and longitude, but out of myself."

Traveling gave me the opportunity to have a look around, to work out where to begin investigating how I got this way. As with all investigations, the challenge is to recognize which avenues of inquiry are likely to be fruitful; to have an instinct for the story before its details have become apparent.

And so I ease myself into the world of crosswords. I meet many of the setters. I hear their stories. I meet even more solvers. The setters seem to me, on the whole, to be more interesting than the solvers. Having found, to my satisfaction, that it is possible to know Rufus, I start looking for the back story to the puzzles and clues that appear every day in our national press.

Remember Chomsky and his appearance in clue in January 2002? The clue was this "Linguist and Philosopher opposed to Vietnam War writing in prison (7)," and like all good clues there was a back story. I arranged to meet the setter, Pasquale, in a pub near Waterloo Station.

Pasquale is a friendly, gentle man who works for the Oxford University Press. Like Rufus, he is known for his prodigious output of puzzles and claims to "set a clue every three hours or so," including sleeping hours! I am eager to meet him because of his puzzles.

But I also want to meet him because he is one of the few people to have criticized Araucaria in print. By now I know enough to appreciate just how highly regarded Araucaria is in the field. Pasquale's particular criticism is that Araucaria strays too far from the rules and is sometimes guilty of grammatical unsoundness. He is, the accusation goes, prone to creating clues that could only be clues, clues in which the surface meaning is too far removed from everyday usage. The clues sometimes make little sense other than as crossword clues. That said, like everyone else he enjoys doing Araucaria's puzzles, especially for his flair both in grid construction and in theme.

Pasquale is a setter on several national papers, but he also edits the puzzles of the *Church Times*, for which Araucaria sets.

"I don't do it much any more," Araucaria tells me. "He keeps changing my clues, which I don't much like."

"Of course," he says, "we have had a long-standing war over this. I did criticize his Ximenean stance some time back. But really I have won that argument to my complete satisfaction."

When I meet Pasquale for supper, it is a foul day. A wet westerly wind is lashing the Thames. He has a ready smile and an impish crinkle to his eyes. We start our discussion by talking about the impact of the September 11, 2001, attacks on New York and Washington. He tells me that in a recent *Times* puzzle the editor took out "assassination" and Pasquale replaced it with "domestication," for which the clue was "What could make wild cat one so timid (13)." The *Times* is not alone in fearing to offend in the wake of tragedy. Pasquale tells me that, following the events of September 11, the editor of the *Independent* reset a corner of a puzzle so as not to have to include the word "airstrike." The *Guardian* is the most lenient of the papers, and does, for example, allow the names of living people. One *Guardian* setter, however, has a terrible record in bringing misfortune on those whose names he has used in the puzzle. Screaming Lord Such, for example, a comedian and musician and a regular participant in British general elections, died the day after the *Guardian* devoted a puzzle to him. One reader spotted this trend and wrote asking never to have a puzzle themed on him. Some publications, of course, take pride in such coincidences. *Private Eye*, the satirical magazine, boasted during the 2002 World Cup that "Clue 11 across in the *Eye* crossword last issue proved spookily prescient for England's footballers. As Cyclops [the setter] wrote: 'Seaman's in: manages to gather one ball, then is a complete waste of time (4-5, 6).'"* Shortly after the clue appeared, England was knocked out of the competition after a lackluster display against Brazil.

In our pub south of the Thames, I ask Pasquale about his criticism of Araucaria, and his face lights up. "I've got the prize puzzle," he says, "on Saturday. Have a look at it. It has a secret message. It's my comment on some of Araucaria's clues." All the broadsheet papers offer prizes for those who solve their Saturday puzzles, which are usually slightly more difficult than those that appear on weekdays. The prize puzzle in the *Guardian* is most often set by Araucaria, but sometimes others get a look in, and they love it when they do. Bunthorne may have one a month. Enigmatist from time to time. Occasionally Paul. And now Pasquale.

Since he has already appeared in print and on the radio commenting on Araucaria's clues, this strikes me as a little coy. I ask him to tell me more, but he won't. "Do the puzzle," he says. And then, as all setters do from time to time, he has a moment of doubt about the clue. "It's a quotation," he adds, "a bit obscure. But it is in the dictionary. I think people will get it. I think it will be all right."

"All right" is an expression setters use frequently. It is a euphemism for "fair."

---

*FART-ARSES AROUND, made up of "Seaman's" = TARS inside "manages" = FARES followed by "one" = A and "ball" = ROUND. David Seaman was England's goalkeeper during the match, and his mistake let in Brazil's winning goal. From *Private Eye* 1057, July 11, 2002.

And so I get the paper and look eagerly for the clue. The clue that appeared in the *Guardian* in January 2002 was this: "See cluer's use of rare, silly pseudo-lingo—absurd nonsense from 4 (10,5,5,5,9)." From time to time the *Guardian* will carry very long anagrams that stretch over the grid, and this is one of them. And I can see the reprimand. Silly pseudo-lingo and all that. But the quote?

I have a moment of doubt. If this is to be a good clue, then the solution and the surface meaning must feed each other. It will not do for the answer to have nothing to do with "cluers" and their (alleged) "silly pseudo-lingo." It must somehow relate. It must somehow complete the story.

And when I get it, of course, it does.

First we need to deal with "4." The answer to 4 down in this puzzle is Chomsky (see Chapter 9). So we can put that into the clue: "See cluer's use of rare, silly pseudo-lingo—absurd nonsense from Chomsky (10,5,5,5,9)." Something Chomsky said, then, and an anagram indicated by "absurd."

The answer is "Colourless green ideas sleep furiously," an anagram of "See cluer's use of rare, silly pseudo-lingo."

This, many *Guardian* solvers will know, is the sentence with which Noam Chomsky announced his arrival as a force to be reckoned with in the field of linguistics. It was the example he chose to demonstrate that a sentence might be grammatical without being meaningful. And we can take it to be a rule for crossword setters too. In a crossword, a clue must say what it means, though it might not mean what it says. But it must mean something. It is not enough for it to be grammatical.

The reprimand is complete.

"Good grief," says Araucaria when I ask him. "Was that about us? I did solve the puzzle—I don't always—but it passed me by completely."

Perhaps, then, the clue is not so very complete. A setter can only set the clue. It takes the solver to complete its meanings, and the meanings are different for each of us. The clue itself will have only one answer, but the associations that each solver can bring to that answer are as many and varied as there are solvers.

Many setters like to include self-referential clues in their puzzles, if only for their own amusement. Often they involve pseudonyms of the setters themselves. Paul, in the *Guardian*, recently came up with "Whoever wrote this dog's dinner's round the bend (4)." The answer, of course is "Paul," meaning "whoever set this." It is made up of a dog's dinner (PAL, a popular brand of dog food in the UK) around "u," which is a well-known plumbing "bend." Similarly, a recent puzzle by *Rover* in the *Guardian* included the pseudonyms of six setters, prefaced with the following warning: "Solutions to the six asterisked clues are of a kind and have no definition."[22]

In the summer of 2001 I was sitting at the kitchen table looking at this puzzle.

My heart sank. I like a clue that has definition. I like, if I'm honest, a clue I can solve. I like a clue that stretches the rules up to, but not beyond, my ken. In my experience, clues that need prefacing go too far, and I want to get on the telephone and say, as my father used to say, "Stop playing silly buggers."

"Oh, you silly bugger," says my girlfriend, interrupting my erudite train of thought. I looked up to see that my son had spilled milk all over his sister's certificate from the Elite Sports Academy, which is how the local school markets itself during the summer holidays.

"I was trying to get the cornflakes," says my son.

"He was flicking them," says my younger daughter. "At you," she adds, catching my eye. My younger daughter understands how adding a little definition can change everything.

If there is no definition, then all the clues will have is the constituent parts of the answer. Where a puzzle has several such clues, the secret is to work out the pattern, to work out what it is that the six clues have in common. At first glance, it appeared that this would be reasonably unproblematic in this crossword. "Castro, with the heart of a lion (7)" gave an early indicator. "Fidelio!" I say with satisfaction, taking the two letters in the middle of "lion" and adding them to the end of Castro's first name. I know that Fidelio is an opera. Clearly, I think, the common link, the missing definition that makes them "of a kind," will be opera.

"What's Fidelio?" asks my younger daughter.

"It's an opera," I say, still pleased with myself, "by Beethoven. In English it's called 'Conjugal Love.'"

"Huh?" says my elder daughter, who is practicing to be a teenager.

"Ask your mother what it means," I reply, returning to the puzzle.

My girlfriend shrugs expressively as she wipes up the milk. If

I didn't know her better, I would think she didn't believe in conjugal love.

The next asterisked clue is similar in structure. "Car behind empty garage (6)"* fairly swiftly yields "Gemini."

Gemini? What the hell has Gemini to do with Fidelio? Was there an opera called Gemini? Was a character in Fidelio called Gemini?

My girlfriend has no view on whether Gemini is an opera.

"Tracy's a Gemini," says my eldest, referring to the friend of a friend, of whom my girlfriend and I slightly disapprove.

So I try another one: "River maiden, perhaps (5)."† Ah, well, that was easy. Only the day before, the *Independent* had used "maiden" in a cricketing sense to mean "over" (it's a summer thing), and "river" commonly serves to indicate R, and so I was quickly onto "Rover."

And then I had it. These were not stars or operas or constellations. These were *Guardian* crossword compilers. The setter was indulging himself.

But at least I had it, and the others—there were six in all—soon followed. Bunthorne, Hendra, and—of course—Araucaria.

It's an old trick and one the compilers love. Fawley, who used to set for the *Guardian*, although he has now moved on to the more austere world of the *Times*, set the 22,000th puzzle for the *Guardian*. In it he managed to use, as part of the clues, no

*GEMINI. The car is a "mini," which comes after GE—an "empty" g[arag]e.
†ROVER. R as in "river," followed by "over" as in what might (perhaps) be a maiden; in cricket the bowler bowls a "maiden" if no runs are scored off six consecutive balls.

less than twenty-six setters' pseudonyms. They make an odd list: Araucaria, Cinephile, Fidelio, Rover, Bunthorne, Hendra, Janus, Taupi, Mercury, Rufus, Auster, Audreus, Pasquale, Chifonie, Paul, Logodaedalus, Orlando, Shed, Gordius, Enigmatist, Egoist, Gemini, Quantum, Crispa, Plodge, Custos. With the exception of Custos, these are the people who had set the two thousand puzzles since the *Guardian* reached the 20,000 mark.

Regular solvers of the *Guardian* puzzle would have recognized all those names, and each name would have had an emotional impact. Some of the clues are quite remarkable tributes to much-missed men. Alec Robins, for example, who set for the *Guardian* as Custos, was remembered thus: "Tailpiece—recollect Custos, so sadly missed (4)." The answer is "SCUT," and the tribute is in the clue, an anagram of CUST(os), the "os" of "so" having been, like Alec Robins himself, "sadly missed."

As with all puzzles, some of the clues require a degree of specialist knowledge—knowledge that I do not yet always have. Take "Does Rufus sometimes substitute his second definition? (7)."* In addition to the obvious merit of getting a setter's name into a clue, this both demands of the reader a certain familiarity with English history and offers a commentary on the layered process of compiling cryptic crosswords.

For Fawley the whole puzzle—like this book— is a tribute to

---

*WILLIAM. To solve this you need to know that King William II (1057–1100) was also known as "William Rufus," or "William the Red," and that "Rufus" is sometimes therefore used in place of "second."

"the *Guardian*'s setters in acknowledgement of all the pleasure they have given me as a solver."[23]

Clueing pseudonyms can be fun; so is choosing them. The late John Perkin, for thirty-eight years editor of the *Guardian* crossword, told me that he introduced them "both as a promise and a warning to the readers," who would know what was coming. By contrast, John Grant, for many years editor of the *Times* crossword (and managing editor of the whole paper), rejected pseudonyms just as he rejects the "cult of personality" they imply. "The whole point," he told me, "is to create a *Times* crossword, not a crossword by someone special that the *Times* happens to carry. We want to be consistent." The current editor of the *Times* feels this burden. In the absence of a pseudonym, the editor cannot hide. The standard of the puzzle is down to him only, and, as a consequence, he is sure he has to edit more heavily than the editors of, say, the *Guardian*, the *Independent*, or the *Financial Times*.

Behind each pseudonym there is not only a person but also a story. Araucaria, for example, is a type of tree known colloquially as a monkey puzzle, which is why the setter chose it. What is perhaps less obvious is why he chose Cinephile as his pseudonym for the *FT*. He chose Cinephile not because he loves movies, but because another name for monkey puzzle is chile pine, of which Cinephile is an "anagram-cum-spoonerism."

Of course it is.

The longer Araucaria goes on, of course, the more apposite it becomes that he chose a pseudonym that is the name for an *evergreen* tree.

In the same Rover puzzle, I came across another clue that made me think again of my father. My father was born in Kirkcaldy in Scotland, on the northern shores of the Firth of Forth, but since being shipped to South Africa in 1939 he has preferred to declare his love for the heather from the safety of a warm climate with a more lenient tax regime. The Harris tweed jacket he bought in 1946 has been worn perhaps twice in fifty years.

"Where reluctant Scotsman lives? (7)"*

Lothian.

I get it, though I am no longer reluctant.

---

*The question mark indicates a witticism of some sort. Reluctant is "loth" and "Ian" is commonly defined as "Scotsman" in crossword puzzles. Lothian is, of course, the area around Edinburgh.

the
river

It is with my familiarity with the rules of crosswords complete that I find myself in the Democratic Republic of Congo.

Normally in the British and American press this is referred to as "the war-torn Congo." If the journalist writing about it has a missionary zeal, he may refer to the war-torn Congo as "the former Zaire," and he may mention that once it was ruled—and plundered—by the colonial power Belgium. He will almost certainly make a passing, and inaccurate, reference to Conrad's *Heart of Darkness*.

If his zeal is great he may also mention Mobutu Sese Seko.

This is as much as any of his audience are likely to know about the Congo. He has, in his zeal, touched all their buttons.

In the war-torn Congo, formerly ruled by Mobutu Sese Seko, we landed on an airstrip littered with the ruined fuselages of MiG fighters. There are helicopters too, and piles of bombs. I am sure there is a technical name for them, but to me they look exactly how bombs should look. They are big and fat, and each has a detonator at one end and a fantail arrangement at the other. Later, we saw the remains of just such bombs in the playing fields of a school in Libenge. The MiG fighters and the bombs were abandoned there when the rebel fighters came in, and now parts of the fuselages provide roofs for the traders who sell mangos and maize by the side of the road.

A television crew and I are traveling down a river, to the front. Like many fronts in many wars, this front is a matter of imagination and of will as much as a matter of fact. The front to which we are heading lies between the troops of the government of Laurent Kabila and the troops of the Movement for the Liberation of the Congo, the MLC.

The river is the Ubangi. It is one of the tributaries of the great Congo River. It rises in the highlands of the Rift Valley to the east and flows more or less west in a gentle arc. It is navigable some distance upstream of Bangui, the capital of the Central African Republic.

I need not tell you that a name like Ubangi is pregnant with possible clues. But let me tell you about the journey to the front. Unlike most journeys, it appears to have neither a beginning nor an end. It has only a middle; an extended, interchangeable, episodic yet relentless middle.

On the night in question, the Ubangi River, which at this

point forms the border between the Democratic Republic of the Congo and the Congo, is wide and glassy, so much so that it is possible to see the Southern Cross, Orion, Castor, Pollux, and other southern-hemisphere friends, reflected in its cumbersome stillness. I say "southern-hemisphere friends," but even as I write it, I realize that it is now more than twenty-five years since I first lay on my back and gazed at the stars of the southern hemisphere. My girlfriend lay next to me and affected interest, which had the interesting—but from her point of view unfortunate—effect that I went away and learned more names of more stars and shared them with her the following night. After which she no longer affected interest.

As we move down the river, the night, like the day, is heavy with moisture and heat. I am on the roof of the boat, surrounded as always by the throb of the outboard motor, through which I can hear the forest and the gentle murmur of soldiers. The night is dark, this being the week of the new moon, but the trees and the guns and the people are vaguely visible, like outlines from a memory.

I am reminded of my girlfriend, and of Robert Frost's homage to the United States, to the land "vaguely realizing westward," which is precisely what the river is doing beneath me. For, as I say, this is a story that has only a middle, and we have moved both ways along the river, and so in this narrative all places and directions and sequences are reversible and interchangeable. In one direction Zambi preceded Dongo, but not in the other, just as in my memory the chronology of this trip is uncertain. There were times when night preceded day, but at other moments it seemed that the days came first and gave way, gracefully through lemon skies, to the gathering night. We seemed always to be on the edge of a gathering night.

In this sense the Ubangi is not like the Batha in Chad. Although it is possible to move both ways within the river, the river itself flows only to the sea. I see now that this is how crosswords work. We worry back and forth amidst the clues, but in the end there is only one answer.

There is only one way to go, only one place to be.

In the end you are who you are.

With the clammy night around me I am on the roof of the boat, realizing a vague longing, as it were, to be with my girlfriend, and I go below, fetch the satellite phone, and settle back on the roof with it. Others can strip and assemble their guns in the dark. After a few days in the Congo I can set up a satellite phone by touch alone. These are new skills for me, like how to cook cassava or kill a crocodile.

The phone is a little miracle. You turn it on, and it searches the night sky for a satellite with which to correspond. By now I know where they are. There is one to the east, at about 45 degrees, and one to the west, at an elevation of 60 degrees. But I like the way the phone flashes up the message "searching for satellite," and so I start in the north, and let the dish gradually swing southward to where I know it will find its mate.

I am reminded of another Rufus clue, perhaps his best. "Swirling mist hides the way forward (8)."*

On this warm night on the Ubangi, my satellite phone finds the satellite. A question flashes up. Do I accept this satellite? I push a button to indicate that I do. Then there follows a delicate and (under other circumstances) frustratingly slow process called "spot beam selection." I have yet to learn what this is, but I like it too. While the machine chugs and whirs, my mind conjures up a hundred cartoon images of spot beams being selected. Soon the spot beam is selected and a new message appears. "Dial 00, country code and number."

I do. I press "call." There are further processes, and the machine is trained to take me through each step. The last stage is "ringing," and I clamp the phone to my ear and let this miraculous sound mingle with those of the forest and the outboard engines. And then there is a fourth, even more miraculous and magical sound, the clear sound of my girlfriend's gentle, lilting, loving voice 5,000 miles away.

She and I talk in low tones. As the boat follows the glorious wide bands of the river, I have to keep the satellite dish facing the right, which is to say eastern, satellite. And so, with the phone to my ear, I hold the dish in both hands and move it in the mirror image of the path of the river. When the boat goes left, I move right. When the boat moves right, I swivel to the left.

And even within this, the pattern is more delicate. For the boat follows not the path of the river banks, which are my ref-

*IMMODEST. Anagram of MIST around MODE = "way," meaning "forward."

erence points, but the path of the deepest channel, which is altogether a different thing, and which the boat pilot seems to
know better than his age. The navigable channel tends to follow the outside curve of the river, which means that the distance traveled is much longer than the distance on the map.
But sometimes this changes and we find ourselves cutting through
the inside edge, the tall banks above us overhung with green.
And, just occasionally, the pilots are consumed by doubt and
slow down enough to take soundings with a long pole, calling
out their findings in voices that slide across the water like a
puck on ice.

I hardly need to say it, do I? Crosswords. I am in love with the
image of the satellite phone searching for its mate. I am in love
with the sense of possibility this idea holds, and with the way it
describes perfectly the relationship between a crossword puzzle
and each solution. I am in love with the idea that just as the
satellite needs a phone to make sense of its being there at all, so
the puzzle needs each solver to complete its meanings. And the
meanings, like the phone calls, are always different, even if the
technical processes are the same. I am in love with the exten-
sions of this idea, in love with the notion of a world made of
such fragile connections.

Crossword puzzles hold us together just as surely as do telephone conversations. The satellite phone and its gossamer
technology, and puzzles and their spiderwebs of associations,
both bind us in to what we know, and who we are. As I float

down the Ubangi River, surrounded by guns and veterans of several wars, I have the strongest sense yet of who I am and where I belong. Tennyson, on behalf of Ulysses, coined the phrase "I am a part of all that I have met . . ." I have a sense somehow that this must be turned on its head. All that I have met is a part of me, and I have been lucky to meet so many, and so much.

And so as my girlfriend and I speak on the satellite phone I am aware that life piles on life, and layer on layer, to produce this delicate filigree through which her voice drifts, a rich, warm, and living presence, and laughter in the air.

I am aware too as we speak that I am on display, lit by the green lights of the satellite phone, and that in the gloom around me curious eyes watch and wonder. It is also possible (and cheaper) for her to phone me, and when she does, the process has an added tension. For the lights on the phone light up before the ringing starts, and for a long second it is not certain at all that the ringing will begin. I answer it before it has a chance. Buttons pressed in Europe can turn off lights in Africa.

As we travel down the river, I am reminded of the debate over the nature of rules in crossword puzzles. I stumbled into this, rather by accident, when comparing my discussions with Pasquale with those I enjoyed with Araucaria. I am reminded how Araucaria used "us" when I told him about the reprimand contained in "Colourless green ideas sleep furiously." "Good grief," he said, "was that about us?"

His use of "us" is instructive. It speaks of a school of setters (of which he, Paul, and Enigmatist are the leading practitioners) for whom rigid adherence to the rules laid down from time to time by those who like rules is really not the point. The point is to stretch the rules. The point is to live not within the rules per se, but within the limits of knowing consent. The point is fully to exploit the play allowed by the steering wheel of the car while always, of course, remaining on the road. Arrayed against such "free" spirits are the custodians of a more disciplined approach to crosswords. It seems to me now that we find these echoes everywhere, in politics, in relationships, in life. Scott, for example, writes that "Common law, as an institution, owes its longevity to the fact that it is not a final codification of legal rules, but rather a set of procedures for continually adapting some broad principles to novel circumstances."[24] The same applies to crosswords. If the solver can reasonably get the answer, and know, having got it, that it is the right answer, then this is enough.

In the Congo there is a war on, and guns surround us.

On the boat we sleep on the roof surrounded by guns. On the plane we kick loaded magazines out the way to make space for our feet. At the hospital where the rebel "minister of health" removed two ovarian cysts from the wife of the sous-commandant of the front-line town, the guns lined the operating theater and in the storm gutter there were spent cartridges that not even the rainy season had been able to wash away.

But this is not surprising. We are traveling through—or per-haps with—a war zone. We carry the wherewithal of war—the people, the weapons, the reason—with us (and again that is reason as cause and reason as motive). For this is a war of sto-ries, and each soldier, as I have said, has his or her story.

At Zambi, for example, a small town some hours down-stream from Bangui, we are joined by "Bra" Doc, splendid in uniform, sneakers, and baseball cap, who works in military in-telligence. But Bra Doc has done the militarily unintelligent thing of going AWOL. He has now repented this error and is returning of his own accord to his unit at the front. Bra Doc, when he joins us, is full of bravado and keen to talk to the tele-vision crew, seeing in us some hope of safety. But it is a forlorn hope, and things don't work out for Bra Doc. Farther down-stream, at Imesse, they court-martial him, beat him until he bleeds, and strip him of all but the baseball cap and a fear-enriched pair of underpants.

Bra Doc looks past me with blank eyes as he staggers onto the boat when it turned to go back upstream. He will, he mum-bles, explain later. He takes his place on a pile of empty flour sacks beside some live crocodiles that we carry for meat. Croc-odiles can survive several days without eating, and the people here therefore prefer to kill them only shortly before they are eaten. Keeping them alive means the meat does not go bad. Once they are captured, therefore, their tails are tied in their mouths, and people carry them slung over an arm like hand-bags. Once back on the boat, Bra Doc never says another word

to me. Instead he sits silent in a corner with the bound crocodiles and weeps, and I have no way of knowing whether his
silence is out of shame, or because he can not really speak
through the congealing mess that had once been his mouth.

Bra Doc leaves us again in Zambi. At least I think so, but
really all I know is that in the morning he is no longer there.
No one has paid much attention, for that was the night of the
storm, when the boat and my imagination both took leave of
their moorings.

But not all stories were like Bra Doc's. Luc, the Third
Battalion commander, appears genuinely glad to get back to
"his boys" at the front, and he presents his sick leave as a
nuisance, something that prevents him from doing what he
does best.

C'est la guerre.

But when we ask Luc when the war will end, he is surprised
that we should inquire at all, and even more surprised that we
appear to think there might be an answer.

From the roof of the boat on the river it is possible to see Orion,
the Southern Cross, the Bear, the Big Dipper, and Sirius, the
dog star. I am surprised it has taken me this long to realize that
I am lying between two worlds. The river is a little north of the
equator, but not much, and I am pretty much equidistant between the place of my birth and the place I call home.

The rebels we have come to film are involved in a slow and

mean war in which hundreds of thousands, perhaps millions, of people are dying. These people are not dying from gunshots or weapons. They are dying of starvation. The rebel leaders are not ideologues. They are primarily businessmen, concerned to make the most of the opportunity that presents itself. They are the children of a previous generation of businessmen, the ones who reaped the harvest of the Mobutu years. They were born in Africa, but they grew up in Europe, as befits the children of the elite. And now they have houses and wives, children and savings in Europe. But their hearts, and their sense of the main chance, are in Africa. And so here they are living remote lives, waiting for history. Some time after we filmed them, this group of rebels made a deal with the government and moved back to Kinshasa. Such are the levels of paranoia, though, that they now have guards to taste their food, and they are afraid to go out at night.

But at the time we are filming them, they too are connected to the world by satellite phone.

Their aerials are lined up, a long row of them, on the balcony of the bullet-scarred former bank building in which they live in Gbadolite. At night, we sit and talk over the rebellion. Some of our discussion is in English; some is in French. I am intrigued to hear the way the language of the French revolution has taken on a new life in this remote place. I am intrigued to hear how "equality" and "liberty" are the stated goals of this struggle. "The people expect nothing less," says one rebel leader, while downstairs his guards play cards and invent sick cousins to tell us about, hoping we will give them a dollar or two to pay for medicines which do not, in any case, exist here.

I have no idea whether the rebels are heroes or not, and I find this disturbing. Downstairs in his office, the secretary-general of the rebel movement is looking at drawings. He is mulling over a number of designs that have been put to him for the new flag of the movement. "We need a symbol," he explains. "We need something that tells people who we are." The pictures do not, at first glance, tell me who he is. They contain the usual symbols of rebel movements in Africa. There are some with the rising sun. There are others with the great river, or the Southern Cross. There are the bright and verdant colors of tropical Africa: blue for water, green for the earth, black for the people, gold or yellow or orange for the mineral wealth. These images have been designed for him in Paris by the son of a friend who is studying art. The friend is also Congolese, but, like the secretary-general, he has another life in Europe.

I am more interested in the words he uses. He tells me that the people are "simple," but that they are not "stupid." He tells me that the rebel leaders have to earn the people's trust. He tells me that he is a Christian Socialist, but that his leader is a "man of the right." He uses terms like "broad umbrella" and "unity" as though they mean something.

He has a visceral sense of the power of images in the service of these words, yet despite the array of images before him he cannot find one that tells the people who he is.

"I wonder," he says. "I think we shall have to improvise."

One night a storm lashes Gbadolite, the town where the rebels have their headquarters. The horizontal rain heads across Independence Avenue and into the maw of Mobuto Sese Seko Avenue. I watched a perfect drop of rain shoot, like a bullet, through a bullet hole in the glass window of my room.

Over a meal, the rebels tease me for being English. "Come back to Africa," they say, "where you belong." But they do not mention their own escape routes, the wives and children, villas, cars and bank accounts safely stowed in Europe. Nor do they mention the daily set of improvisations they make in order to bring some continuity to their fractured purpose.

To leave the Congo involves a series of implausible journeys. I have an image of myself crouched in a pirogue, crossing the river. With me are a Lebanese businessman and his security people. They are carrying a huge bag of cash. The security people tell me they are ex-Hezbollah. They have fled the conflict in southern Lebanon, which is what they call "home." Across the river we spend the night in the deserted house of another Lebanese businessman. He has gone, but his satellite TV subscription has not run out. We watch women with big hair read the news in Arabic. That I should be sharing a meal with ex-Hezbollah guerrillas in a border town in the Central African Republic strikes me as unlikely.

Not impossible, but unlikely.

On our way to the airstrip there is an altercation when a group of bandits demands money from us. There are regular reports of banditry in the area. Nuns have been killed for their cars. The businessman and his people appear to regard this as routine. Voices are raised. Guns are discreetly drawn. A man is slapped in the face. The bandits back down. I, the innocent, am a spectator in this drama. I realize that all the other men understand this particular game, but that I do not. I realize that the nature of their understanding is not what I might, under other circumstances, have thought of as a grasp of the rules. Rather it is an understanding that there are no rules. The men with whom I am traveling appear happy to assert their dominance, with or without rules.

I have been away a long time, and I am impatient to return home; I am impatient for England, for the beautiful mess we call London. I am impatient to be home with my girlfriend, where I belong.

It occurs to me that London, like crosswords, lives by rules that are not written, and that are changing, and that I now know how to play the game in which everything is vague, and anything is possible.

When I land at Heathrow, I know what to do.

what
lord archer
ever did
for me

It is not only that when I am in England I know what to do. It is also, I realize, that I understand the stories England tells about itself. I first visited Grantchester in 1987, when friends of mine were students at Cambridge. They lived in a rented house next to the old vicarage, and we would walk through the Grantchester meadows into town, or up the river to Byron's Pool. It was only many years later that I had reason to revisit the village, and to consider how it was that places I had thought of as backdrops were now center-stage. I realize that this is to do with how we tell the story; with how, indeed, we identify that there is a story at all, and it is to do with the layers we are able to bring, as it were, to the party. Take, for example, four events that are connected only through a crossword clue:

In 1912, Rupert Brooke, the English poet, wrote a poem.

In 1953, Araucaria won a competition.

In 1987, the (now) Lord Jeffrey Archer told a lie.

In 2001, Nick Smith of Oxfordshire wrote a letter to the
Guardian.

These men have never met, yet they share a story.

Rupert Brooke's poem "The Old Vicarage, Grantchester" is
a typical act of nostalgia on his part, which, along with warm
beer and old ladies on bicycles (John Major's uniquely erotic
evocation of England, our England) has assumed a central place
in the stories England tells about itself. Brooke wrote the poem
while on a visit to Berlin, and it is filled with an exile's longing
for home, and with images of an English pastoral idyll. Few, I
would think, now could quote from the poem, except perhaps
the last two lines:

Stands the Church clock at ten to three?
And is there honey still for tea?

But many will know the title, and will know that Rupert
Brooke once lived at the Old Vicarage and heard from his win-
dow the babbling Cam slipping across the meadows toward
Cambridge. They will know also that a certain Lord Archer, fa-
mously, now lives in the Old Vicarage in Grantchester, outside
Cambridge, with his wife, Mary. Those who know this will

know also that Lord Archer has literary pretensions and is not above associating himself with Brooke. His house in Grantchester has a blue plaque saying that the poet once lived there too.

Brooke, through the mixed fortunes of good looks and an early death (from blood poisoning en route to war service in the Dardanelles), has long been a symbol of romantic patriotism, and his becoming such was hastened by the posthumous publication of several works, including "The Soldier," whose famous first line ("If I should die, think only this of me . . .") is now a staple of English identity. Given that he was already dead by the time the poem was published, the line took on a weight and life in excess of anything it might have merited on purely literary grounds. Many will know that, although he owns the Old Vicarage, Grantchester, Lord Archer does not always stay there. His writing career has brought him great wealth, and he owns several properties. For example, he sometimes stays at his penthouse overlooking the Thames, and he has used it sometimes to entertain women not his wife. They will know also that this has, on occasion, gotten him into trouble with the popular press, the Conservative Party hierarchy, and the law. And, one assumes, with his wife, although she is discreet, and so one can only assume.

Araucaria is now an old man, but he continues his prodigious output of fifteen crosswords each month, as he has for forty-five years. He is, as we know, no disciple of crossword disciplinarians like Ximenes, but he is a stylist, and his reputation for fiendish complexity is matched only by his reputation for fairness, which is to say he will not knowingly cut corners in a clue. Every letter will have its purpose, and every purpose its letter. "They are building blocks," he says, "the building blocks of the imagination. If you don't understand that, you can't hope to understand crosswords."

Consider then, the clue that Nick Smith, in his letter to the *Guardian* on January 21, 2001, claimed to be "the best cross-word clue ever." Nick, a publisher of academic journals, lives with his wife and two small children in an Oxfordshire village. A county bridge player, he is also a fanatical crossword solver and estimates he has, in his time "done" 10,000 puzzles. He has, therefore, some basis on which to make such an assessment.

Consider two more pieces of information that would have been readily available to *Guardian* readers like Nick. The first is that in 2000, thirteen years after he told it, Jeffrey Archer's lie came back to haunt him. He had, at the time, in order to deny press speculation about his sex life, claimed to have spent a particular night in the company of a friend, thus rendering impossible certain newspaper claims that he had spent the night in question in the company of a prostitute. He had, further, inveigled the friend to confirm this lie on his behalf. But, thirteen years later, the friend chose, as they say, to spill the beans, and as I write, Lord Archer is in prison, convicted of perjury and of perverting the course of justice.

The second piece of information is that there was a time, after these revelations were made and before his subsequent trial and conviction, during which he retired from the public eye, and in particular from his campaign to be come Mayor of London, and took refuge in the Old Vicarage, Grantchester.

And so to the clue: "Poetical scene has surprisingly chaste Lord Archer vegetating (3,3,8,12)." The answer—the solution, perhaps—is "The Old Vicarage, Grantchester," a "surprising" anagram of "chaste Lord Archer vegetating," or as Nick Smith put it to me, the most "perfect clue, probably the best ever."

Why? Those who don't do crossword puzzles may think this a small point. But those who do will know that legitimate twenty-six-letter anagrams are few and far between. They will know that clues that call on such a range of knowledge for their solution come along only now and then. They will have experienced the tedium of simple anagrams, and will have dismissed simpler references to the English poetic tradition. And they will know that, somewhere in this clue—and in the puzzle that surrounded it, for the theme of the day was English verse—a particular kind of genius is at work, and that we are the lucky ones, to witness it.

I asked Araucaria to re-create for me the process of creating this clue. Although he has now acquired a computer and may on occasion use it, he prefers to do his anagrams with an old scrabble set. He spills the pieces onto the table in the sitting room of his small house, and spells out "the Old Vicarage Grantchester" before scraping the rest of the pieces back into their box. As he does so I detect a change in him. From being a shy and quiet-spoken man, he takes on a mantle of authority. The set of his mouth changes. His fingers caress the scrabble pieces, and I notice that some of the pieces are so worn that he has had to ink in the letters again. "Is that your original set?" I ask. He is not sure. I decide that for the sake of the story it must be.

"'Lord Archer' came first," Araucaria[25] told me with a twinkle, and he removes from the jumble of letters the ones that make up the two words. "And he had been in the news a lot. He's always in the news. I think they call it a 'flair for publicity.'" He pauses and moves the letters around on the rosewood coffee table. "And I thought it would be interesting to do something with Lord Archer." But I can see that he is not really thinking about me, nor about Archer. His mind is calculating other anagrams, his fingers dancing from one to another like a jazz pianist groping for a song. And I have a sense of his absolute certainty that the song is in there, and that it will emerge, given the time and the place.

Or, perhaps, given the artist.

"But it didn't leave me much," he says, a little affronted that he should be left with so poor a selection of letters. Those that remain are T,H,E,V,I,C,A,G,E,G,A,N,T,E,S,T. "Not very much at all." Again he casts his hands across them, mixing times and keys, playing snatches from forgotten clues.

"At first I got the word 'teach,' and I was trying to think what to do with 'teach.' And of course I had 'ing.' But 'teach' or 'teaching' didn't lead anywhere. What have they to do with Archer? So the clue only came when I worked out that I could have 'chaste.' And I knew immediately that 'chaste' and 'Lord Archer' could make something interesting. And so I took 'chaste' out"—which he does as he speaks—"and I was left with this lot." And he looks down at these letters, and again I notice the twinkle in his eye: T,E,V,I,G,E,G,A,N,T. "And then I had it." It occurs to me, as he says this, that Nick Smith wrote his psychology doctorate on the subject of what Aristotle called *anagnorisis*, the moment of discovery that forms the thin blue line between knowledge and ignorance. And it occurs to me— which it had not done before—that this applies as much to setters as to solvers.

Araucaria and I look at each other, and I see that the look in his eye is not just a twinkle. There is something else there, a suggestion of sterner stuff, and a knowledge that he is straying into territory where only the braver setters go. He is making a political statement. He is delivering a reprimand to Lord Archer and all his vain dishonest ilk, and he is doing it in the most delicate, most imaginative manner possible. And in doing so he is giving rein to a notion of romance and of patriotism to which I do not believe Lord Archer can begin to aspire.

There are many layers to this clue, more than just the serendipity of the anagram, or the topicality. Consider the anagram indicator. We have seen earlier what a variety of words can be used for an indicator. The best ones work when they add to the surface and deeper meanings of the clue. In this case, "surprising" is both the anagram indicator and the word that gives the most bite to the reprimand. We, the solvers, have no idea whether or not Lord Archer is chaste, nor do we much care. But we do laugh out loud to think that we might be surprised by this notion. And the word in its dual role is the perfect choice of anagram indicator. We can imagine Araucaria constructing the clue. Having gotten the anagram, then what? How does he order the words in order to create a meaning? What else does he bring to bear?

We can imagine him making other calculations too. What is the definition? It could—for those really in the know—just have been "at home," since we know that the answer is also the name of Lord Archer's home. But the choice of "poetical scene" adds to the sense of dismay that our public life is polluted by the likes of Archer. After all, this "poetical scene" is part of the national landscape, and part of the national memory, and yet it is better known now as the home of a mendacious and disgraced minor novelist. So the choice of definition and the choice of indicator broaden the meanings of the clue and strengthen the narrative. A perfect choice.

"And when you saw the letter," I ask Araucaria, meaning Nick Smith's letter to the *Guardian*, "were you pleased?"

"The letter? Oh, oh, that letter." He pauses to give the question its due weight, for he is a polite and gentle man. "I think it surprised me. I was just pleased to have got the anagram." He pauses again, and I hear the church bell toll from the village. "But I suppose it is really rather good." And then, as if he has had to persuade himself, he adds "It is good. It has what we all hope for. It has cohesion, and discipline. It has layers. I was pleased with the layers."

I was pleased with the layers too. I was pleased to have reached the point where this all made sense to me, and to be part of the shared experience.

I was pleased to belong, just as my mother's godmother had been pleased to belong in her house in Nairobi all those years before.

The kinds of stories endure. Some months later, after Lord Archer had been convicted of his various offenses and locked away for a four-year prison sentence, a *Guardian* reader in the Netherlands remembered the Araucaria clue and proposed a new clue. "Now that [Lord Archer] has changed addresses," he wrote, "may I suggest an update: 'Where shaken Archer's "I'm noble!" palls' (1,8,6,4)."*

---

*A BELMARSH PRISON CELL, an anagram indicated by "shaken."

falling
in love
again

From time to time, my girlfriend and I find it sympathetic to do the crossword together.

Because I have met so many clues, I no longer admit to having a favorite, but she does. My girlfriend's favorite delivers everything you could ask of a good clue. In fact it delivers it all, and then some. Her choice clue is this:

"Bust down reason? (9)." This was not set by a "professional," but by an amateur and devotee of the Azed puzzle in the *Observer*. The setter is a man called Les May. According to Azed, Les has stopped submitting clues to the competition. Azed speculates that "the missus" delivered an ultimatum to Les: puzzles or me. "But he's still around," Azed adds, "I still see him from time to time."

That question mark is a warning to us all.

Bust. Down. Reason. Question mark. Nine letters.

"Bust" can mean many things. My girlfriend thinks immediately of "décolletage," but that seems a little obvious. It could be a face hewn in rock. It could be an arrest.

Down. Well, "down" can also mean many things. Down is what you get from ducks. Down is blue. Down is not up.

Reason? Would that be reason as cause or reason as motive? Or reason as logic?

The arithmetic alone is intimidating.

Even the 2001 *Concise Chambers Crossword Dictionary* lists twelve meanings for "bust," forty-one meanings for "down," and fifty meanings for "reason."

This is a common problem. Bill Bryson in *Mother Tongue* gives the example of "set." It takes the *Oxford English Dictionary* 60,000 words to define all the meanings of "set." It has fifty-eight uses as a noun, 126 as a verb, and ten as a participial adjective. The arithmetic may be intimidating, but it is also the reason it is so entertaining. It does not help that in English the same word can contradict itself. "Cleave," for example, can mean "to cut in half" or "to stick together." "Left" can mean "departed" or "remaining."

Therefore, let's try another approach. Perhaps it is an "& lit." ("cryptic and literal"), in which the clue is both the whole meaning and the constituent parts. "Bust down reason?" Nine letters.

That question mark troubles my girlfriend. She knows not to trust it. A question mark means that the setter is messing with you. It means he is not being entirely fair, but that you will let him off when you get it.

Let's go back to it as an "& lit." clue. "& lit." means that the whole clue is both the "cryptic clue" and the "definition." So we can look at the clue and try to think what it might literally mean. Bust down reason. Well, when she thinks of it as an "& lit." clue, my girlfriend gets quickly enough to "brainwash," which might reasonably be thought of as a nine-letter word for the process of breaking down a man's reason. Dictionaries define "brainwash" in various ways. Merriam-Webster's (online) dictionary tells us it is "a forcible indoctrination to induce someone to give up basic political, social, or religious beliefs and attitudes and to accept contrasting regimented ideas." It goes on to tell us that this is of Chinese etymology and entered the language after being translated from the Chinese in 1950.

But what's with the question mark?

What's the joke?

What is the cryptic definition? By what other road might we have gotten to the answer?

B. Rain. Wash.

Hmmm.

Bra. In. Wash.

Bra in wash!

One's bra being in the wash may or may not be the "reason" one's "bust" is "down." It is to do with one's décolletage!

Bloody hell!

It is a lovely, lovely clue.

It almost matches my girlfriend's gorgeous life-enhancing laughter. When she solves the clue, her laughter echoes around the house. It cascades down the banisters and bounces off the ceilings. The same glorious décolletage-shaking laugh that has filtered to me down countless phones lines all over the world fills our house to bursting.

My girlfriend maintains she would have gotten the answer sooner, except that she has more than one bra. That a single bra is in the wash would not, of itself, be sufficient reason.

She is of the view that the passage of time and three children played their part.

And me. I was there too.

For once, therefore, I will not take you back.

We are living now in the present.

The story is happening as I write.

There is not long to go.

As I write, I am aware that I have lived nearly half my life in London. My fortieth birthday approaches. A relentless west wind batters my window. The forecast was for rain and gales. We have had rain and gales, and then some. The forecast for this evening is for clear skies. The temperature will plummet.

Snug in my study, I have a sense of being the playmaker. Simply by telling the story, I have solved the mystery of how I came to be this way. We know how it came to be, and the question now is what to do next. I need some help, and so for this I need an accomplice. But who?

For this book I have interviewed perhaps thirty regular setters for the British broadsheet press, several editors, and many solvers. I am interested to know who is the best setter, who is, as it were, the setters' setter.

Bunthorne, of the *Guardian*, is one possibility, but on this, of course, there is no consensus. Pasquale is another. We have seen that there is a distinction between those who rigorously follow the Ximenean protocol and those who do not. As Bunthorne puts it, "Of course, I am a Ximenean. But I know that if it weren't for [Araucaria] pushing the boundaries, the rest of us wouldn't get anywhere at all. I mean that's the thing. You've got to be fair. And you've got to entertain."

I want to be fair, and to entertain.

These are my rules.

In the course of these interviews, it has been my habit to ask setters to tell me their favorite clues. It is typical of Araucaria that when I ask him, he gives the work of two other setters. "Potty Train (4)" and "I say nothing (3)," both clues that derive their excellence from their precision and their brevity. Neither is very hard to solve, however. Neither, it seems to me, delivers the spontaneous explosion of mirth, comprehension, and sheer wonder at the ingenuity of the setter, although "potty train" comes close. A setter, remember, is entering a game in which the point is to lose gracefully. If no one can solve the clue, there is no point to the clue at all. And setters, certainly all the setters I have met, are harsh judges. There are no rules, but they all know the rules. And in amongst the cat-fighting and the criticism, there are occasional moments of genuine appreciation of their art.

Which brings us to Antarctica.

I have not been to Antarctica, but my brother has.

My brother is a scientist, and in his relentless quest to know more and more about less and less, he went to Antarctica in 1992 and again in 1993. There are photographs of him in a red cagoule with snow on his beard. He wears sunglasses and rides about on a Ski-Doo. He knows a lot about the lichens that grow on ice.

At the time my brother is in Antarctica, there appeared in the *Guardian* a clue that now appears in many lists of all-time favorite clues.

It is a gem of a clue.

It concerns Antarctica.

At least it might.

It depends how you read it.

It is the autumn of 2001, and I am in Lancashire, in a small seaside town. I have a decent slug of coffee inside me, I have a page of notes, and I am wandering around Bunthorne's den, where he sets his famously testing puzzles for the *Guardian*. Bunthorne has been setting puzzles since before I was born. He claims to have chosen the name "Bunthorne" only after "Cunnilingus" was rejected by someone at the *Guardian*.

"They had to ask what it was," he chuckles. "Didn't know

people did that." Bunthorne is the name of a character in the operetta *Patience*, and it was deemed, by those at the *Guardian* who deem these things, to be more erudite.

In his study, surrounded by the dictionaries and encyclopedias that are the staple of any setter's workspace, in pride of place above his desk there is a faded and curled postcard. The picture is of a dog.

Bunthorne shows me around his study and finds on his computer a file of favorite clues. Some are his, but many belong to other setters. Some show traces of humor of the sort you might expect from a man whose preferred pseudonym is "Cunnilingus"—"Bearing slash from sword (4)," for example, or "He is understood to have relations (5)," or even "Singers of the lost generation (8)."* But there is one he doesn't draw attention to, except to say that it is his wife's favorite. Nor does he draw my attention to the faded and bent postcard on the wall above his desk. But I notice it anyway. It is out of place amidst the regimental order of the study. I lean over to look at the postcard and notice that it has been much used. There are marks where the drawing pin has been taken out and put in, again and again.

The postcard is from Araucaria.

Bunthorne has been setting puzzles in the *Guardian* since 1961, two years fewer than Araucaria. They are not quite of a generation, for Araucaria is thirteen years Bunthorne's senior. Araucaria

*EPEE, ROGER, and CASTRATI, respectively.

is the son of a bishop, and he has medals to show for his war heroism. Bunthorne has memories of a working-class childhood in Burnley and of a father determined that they would better themselves through learning. To hear him talk of it is to think of Mr. Gradgrind and his obsession with facts.

When I see the clue that Bunthorne offhandedly called his wife's favorite, it seems to me that his forty years of work have become distilled into a single clue, a clue of such brilliance and such humor as to cause us to catch our breath and hoot.

This is Bunthorne's clue: "Amundsen's forwarding address (4)."

Bunthorne describes himself as a working-class journalist and photographer. He is self-educated. He has, therefore, the self-educated man's view that what he knows, it is not unreasonable to expect all other *Guardian* readers to know. Actually, it *is* unreasonable, because he is very well read and remembers most of it. But the theory is sound; the theory that from time to time we articulate. The theory that I long ago applied to my mother's godmother and her friends at their house in the hills above Nairobi. I am reminded of a story told to me by John Grant, for many years the editor of the *Times* crossword. "We used to joke that it was a lonely hearts club," he said, "because we knew that for some of our solvers, it was the one time of the day when they felt in touch with the rest of the world."

Azed, who sets the fiendishly difficult puzzle for the *Observer*, tells an even more poignant story: perhaps 300 people complete and submit the Azed prize puzzle each month, and one of these was a woman whose entries arrived always on time, always immaculately filled in, and almost always correct. Then one day her entries stopped. Azed wondered what had happened to her, but after a couple of weeks he thought no more about it. Some time later he got a letter in a familiar handwriting. "I thought you would like to know," the letter read, "that your correspondent passed away last month." It was from the solver's neighbor, who had filled in the puzzle each week and sent it in. "I can't do them myself," she wrote, "but she was very good. She needed me, you see, because she was blind."

They also serve who only write it down.

In terms of the theory that we belong, and that crosswords are an expression of our belonging, then, it is not unreasonable for Bunthorne to assert that what he knows, other *Guardian* readers might be assumed to know.

It is reasonable to think that most *Guardian* readers will have some idea who Amundsen is. They will know that Amundsen was an explorer, that he reached the South Pole first, and that he was not popular with the great British public, not least because he beat "our" man Shackleton to the South Pole and had the temerity to survive to tell the tale.

The average reader will look at this clue and have firmly fixed in his mind the South Pole and a frostbitten Norwegian.

Amundsen's forwarding address?

Forwarding address?

Where would Amundsen have had his mail sent?

Four letters?

Pole?

Amundsen?

What was Amundsen's first name? Is that what he means by address?

And so on.

Actually, the answer is "mush."

Actually, "forwarding address" refers to what Amundsen might have said to his dogs to make them go forward. "Mush" is what any of us might have said to our dogs to make them go forward. "Mush" is how we address dogs, if we are explorers in Antarctica.

It is a lovely clue.

"Why Amundsen?" I ask Bunthorne, but he is already answering me.

"It had to be him," he says. "Had to be. Because he used dogs, of course."

I look blank.

"Shackleton used a tractor," he says.

Of course.

I say "of course," but a part of me doubts it. I discover—inevitably—that Bunthorne is right. Amundsen did rely on dogs, and talked about them as "my family." If ever there should be a prosecution, this will lead as evidence that the average *Guardian* reader cannot be expected to know everything Bunthorne

knows. The average *Guardian* reader will not know that it had
to be Amundsen.

My brother has spent two summers in Antarctica, and I did
not know that Amundsen referred to his dogs as "our children."
I am willing to wager a month's salary that my brother does not
know that Amundsen claimed that the whole success of the trip
depended on the dogs.

But this is not the point. The point is that this is a beautiful and
poetic clue. It does not mean what it says, but it says what it
means. It creates the most unlikely association; it demands a
leap of imagination from the solver, and—best of all—it delivers the breathtaking moment of realization not just of the answer, but of its own legitimacy.

A vindication of its own legitimacy.

Who can ask for more?

This takes us far beyond Adrian Bell's requirement that
there should be a groan of satisfaction. This is a three-word
apologia pro vita sua.

And this is what Araucaria is acknowledging in the frayed
postcard pinned to the wall of Bunthorne's study in his neat
house in a small Lancashire town.

"Dog shouldn't slobber over dog," it reads, "but I thought
'Amundsen's forwarding address' was <u>wonderful</u>. Araucaria."

I need not tell you just how much Bunthorne treasures this
recognition.

They should put it as his epitaph.

Mush.

As I leave, Bunthorne offers me his own epitaph on crosswords. "It's a very personal thing for me, the *Guardian*. It's all that ever mattered to me, the comfort of there being a group of like-minded people. To belong . . ." His voice trails off, and his gaze goes past me to the windswept expanse of Morecambe Bay.

There are white horses on the water, and a running tide.

the
story
of my
life

In the early winter of 2001, I made up my mind. I wanted a puzzle about me to appear in the *Guardian*, and I wanted Araucaria to set it.

Since this takes memoir to new levels of narcissistic endeavor, I should offer a note of self-deprecation. The late John Perkin told me this clue: "He saw himself as winning on the pools (9)."* I do not think it was a reprimand, although he did mention it almost immediately after I had said how I wanted to be able to have this memoir culminate in a puzzle themed on my story.

When I asked them, both Araucaria and the current *Guardian* editor laughed. To their credit, both understood the idea imme-

*NARCISSUS!

diately. They understood the game. They were interested in the possibilities it held.

I went on. I wanted a puzzle to write about, a puzzle that was somehow about me. I wanted it to be the prize puzzle. And I wanted it to appear on my fortieth birthday.

Will there be anything else?

No, thank you. That will do nicely.

And the words?

I gave Araucaria a list of words. As a theme for the puzzle I chose "thrillers." It had long seemed to me that there was a connection between the way in which the hero of a thriller or detective story will set about solving the crime and the way in which solvers must approach a puzzle. Both must look for previously undiscovered meanings. Both must make the transition from being outside the story to being the center of it. When the hero of a thriller is confronted by the corpse in Chapter 1, he is inclined to believe that the story is about the dead person. But by the end of the book, the story will have moved on. The corpse is forgotten, and the hero is the person who matters. It is up to him to bring matters satisfactorily to a conclusion. It is the same for the solver of crosswords. His interpretations of the clues are what matters. By the end of the puzzle, he has taken a route to solving it that is unique to him. Like the hero of a thriller, he will have overcome obstacles in completing the puzzle.

Quite frequently that obstacle will have been his girlfriend.

And so I gave Araucaria a list of words. He got most of them in, but there were some he left out. He didn't, for example, find a place for "English." Nor did he fit in "previously undiscovered meanings," although of course the puzzle, like all crossword puzzles, is about just such meanings. It is an invitation to you to complete its meaning, to bring to it your own histories, and your own memories. But he did get in "hero" and "Sandy," "thriller," and "autobiography."

And most importantly, he did get in my "girlfriend."

And the grid? Crossword people love symmetry, and so I asked for *Guardian* grid 40, but Araucaria was of the view that this is a lousy grid. Instead he used grid 28. Grid 40 did not offer enough variety of word length. It had only recently occurred to me that the papers must each have a stack of grids of standard arrangements that they use in rotation. In fact, the *Guardian* has fifty designs, but only about forty of them are used. The *Telegraph* has sixty, the *Independent* thirty-three, and the *FT* only sixteen. The *Times* has fifty, but the editor tells me he is re-designing some of them. He is particularly pleased to have designed a grid that has every word length from three to thirteen letters. There are pieces of software now that make it very easy to create and design new grids.

Araucaria set the puzzle over the Christmas break of 2001. While he worked, my girlfriend and I and our children went to Italy. We have friends there who live in a large farmhouse overlooking a valley. The valley is filled with chestnut trees and olive groves. In the bright cold winter evenings the sun sets behind the distant hill, and the full moon rises. The mountain behind us is covered in snow. There are field mice in the pastures.

We take skiing lessons and stroll through cobbled streets. We eat slices of pizza, and we attend Mass in a freezing church where the white clouds of our breath mingle with the incense. The sermon concerns tolerance for refugees. The priest leaps the centuries; there have always been refugees, and Italy has many. He talks about the flight into Egypt, and about the many people now found in the towns of Italy. They come from Nigeria and Kosovo, from Ethiopia and Afghanistan. In the bright light outside the Abbey of Sant' Antimo in Tuscany I find myself wondering whether these émigrés will become Italian.

I wonder what accents their children will have.

In a walled town, our children with their oh-so-north-London accents guard the ramparts of a medieval castle. Since I have brought no books with me, and Italians crosswords demand more than my modest Italian, I am not distracted. My girlfriend and I hold hands and watch distant horizons.

On our friends' farm there is a swing from one of the chestnut trees. It's a simple affair; one I helped erect some ten years before. It consists simply of a car tire suspended on perhaps ten meters of rope. What sets this particular swing apart is that the tree from which it hangs is poised on a very steep earth bank. Just to get to the launchpad takes a few minutes of battling up the slippery slope. But as soon as you are on it, the swing carries you swiftly away from the earth. At its peak you are perhaps fifty feet above the ground.

The children love it. They launch themselves into the crisp evening air and swing up, kicking out to reach the twigs of a distant branch. For them the distant branch marks the high point of the swing's arch.

I look at it another way.

I see that if you swing high enough, you can see beyond the hill on the far side of the valley. Beyond this hill lies the Maremma, the marshlands of southern Tuscany, and beyond that the Mediterranean. If everything lines up just right, if you swing high enough, and the sun is low enough, and the evening clear enough, it is possible to see the sun on the distant sea. The sun breaks through silver clouds and the orange dusty air seems to part, and the light shimmers for a moment, for me. For me the high point is not only to do with height. It is also to do with timing, and with the way the "sudden variousness" of the world combines to produce a moment of magic.

Crossword setters speak often of serendipity, and they will say that part of the skill is to be open to the moment when an idea takes shape. The skill is to let the clue emerge. The skill is one of patience, and of timing, and perhaps—like the swing— of just a little engineering. In a recent puzzle, for example, the setter Paul chose Peru as his theme. Ostensibly, the reason for this was that he used the publication of the puzzle to appeal for funds for a sponsored walk he intends to do through Peru. But part of me—and not least because I now know Paul—suspects that the whole thing was dreamed up to create this clue: "Laughs, with 6 when conspiring (5)." Six down in this puzzle is INCA, as in the Inca Trail. We can therefore rewrite the clue as "Laughs, with Inca when conspiring (5)."

As I looked at this clue, I was reminded of the first time I met Paul. He is the youngest of the *Guardian* setters and has been setting puzzles since 1995. He is a protégé of Araucaria, and tells a wonderful story about the first time he met Araucaria. He had long since decided he wanted to be a setter, and over time he built up a correspondence with Araucaria with a view to honing his skills. One day they agreed to meet at Peterborough station. Araucaria met him, and together they went out to Araucaria's car.

"My heart sank," Paul recalls, "because in that moment I knew that as a crossword setter I was always going to be poor. Here was the best setter in the country, and he was driving a Fiat Panda!"

Paul does not have Araucaria's breadth of knowledge, nor does he have the discipline that comes from a half-century of setting puzzles. People who have been setting puzzles for as long as Araucaria has know what they can get away with. They know what the solvers will accept. They do not necessarily understand rules as a code of practice, but they do understand rules as a form of storytelling, and they know what it means to remain within spitting distance of the main narrative. Paul sometimes strays too far, but he does have moments of genius and a wicked wit. The first time I met him, he was complaining that an editor had rejected one of his clues: "Ancient Hindu in a jiffy (4)."

In one sense this is a simple anagram. But it does not present it-self as an anagram, because the anagram indicator is buried in another word. The indicator is "iffy," and the letters to be used are "in a j." Then, quickly, we get to Jain.

But only because we know.

The complaints were that we did not know, and could not be expected to know, and so the editor rejected the clue. This is an old debate. In his book, Don Manley takes Araucaria to task for using "innate" in the same way in the clue "False clue is in-nate—group round a centre (8)," for which the answer is "NU-CLEATE." The problem, according to Manley, is that there is nothing to indicate that "nate" should be thought of as separate from "in."[26]

I bore this in mind as I looked at "Laughs, with Inca when conspiring (5)."

The answer is "hoots."

Hoots means laughs.

"In cahoots" means conspiring.

Oh, dear.

You can hear Adrian Bell's groan of satisfaction ringing out across the country. You can also hear a grinding of Ximenean teeth. And you can imagine the little bit of engineering that Paul went through to create the grid that allowed the clue. I haven't asked him. For all I know, he regards it as one of his or-dinary clues.

But I doubt it.

And so "my" puzzle came to be in the newspaper. And I real-ized that every puzzle, every clue of every puzzle, not only tells a story, but has a story. I realized that we can take back bearings from any single clue and there will, necessarily, be an invisible thread taking us back through time and memory. Like the travelers in Robert Louis Stevenson's poem, we may only catch of each "a glimpse" before they are "gone forever." Nonetheless they bind to our past and our future, and to each other.

They tell us who we are.

They tell you who you are.

I am fascinated by the idea that each clue not only tells a story, but also has a story. Biologists use this idea. They write about how every single thing represents an end point of a particular evolutionary chain. You and I are as far as evolution has gotten. It need not have happened this way. There could have been many billions of other possible outcomes. But this is the one that happened. It is the same with puzzles. It could have been any puzzle—but it isn't. It is this one, and this is its story.

And so this memoir is really the chronicle of a crossword foretold, the story of how this particular puzzle came to be. Perhaps not all puzzles have such a complicated genesis— except that how can they not? How can there not be, feeding into each clue, each idea, each witticism, a story at least as varied and unpredictable as mine?

Almost all of the words from this particular puzzle have appeared in the book both as the words, and as the clues or versions of the clues. There are a few exceptions. It is in the nature of filling in the grid that the more words you put in, the fewer are the options for the remainder. Eventually, there are some words that simply have to be used to fit in with the rest of the puzzle. "Okapi" occurs in many puzzles for this very reason. If the checked letters are K and P, then "skips" is an alternative. If the checked letters are O, A, and I, however, "okapi" is pretty much the only option. Mention "okapi" to any crossword setter and he will roll his eyes and groan.

They have all been there. Rufus, for example, has clued it five times in his career. In the *Guardian*, he used "A wild animal, but it's all right, a quiet one (5)." In the same paper, Janus recently came up with "Took a piece, or part, of animal (5)."[27] Don Manley exhorts his readers to regard these "fillers" as old friends, rather than as irritants. We have to have them, and we should accept that they are part of the landscape of crosswords.

"Smee" is another example. A "smee" is a kind of duck. There are hundreds of words that fit the pattern "S_E_." But if the checked letters are M and E in the pattern "_M_E," then you either have to go with "smee," or rework the grid. From time to time setters go with "smee."

Both "smee" and "okapi" are animals of which we would know little, were it not for crosswords.

You could say the same of me.

On our return from Italy, Araucaria sends me the puzzle. It arrives in a form I have not previously seen. The clues are on the left side of the page. The solutions are on the right, together with various forms of crossword annotation to explain each answer.

"I hope you think it's all right," he says. "I think it is. I think it should be okay."

It occurs to me that, along with crosswords, Araucaria has long since mastered the art of the understatement.

Forty years after I was born in Johannesburg, the puzzle—my puzzle—appears in the *Guardian*. It is February 16, 2002, and the puzzle is number 22445. I rise early and hurry to the newsstand, where I buy up the entire stock of *Guardians*. I take them home and spread one out on the kitchen table. To forestall a lurking panic attack and to make sure there are no typing errors, I quickly fill in the grid. It all looks fine. I am a little nervous, though. Now that I see it in print, I am not sure whether it will stand the scrutiny of thousands of solvers. Will they spot some glaring error that neither Araucaria, nor I, nor the *Guardian* editor has seen?

I am still gazing at it, with a grin on my face and a certain melancholy in my heart, when the children come down to have their breakfast.

"Happy birthday, Daddy."

"Look," I say, "I'm in the paper."

"Are you? Where?"

They cluster around me, and I show them the grid, complete with my name.

They look disappointed.

"That's not you, Daddy," says my younger daughter. "That's a crossword puzzle."

Children have a way of seeing through things.

But I wasn't prepared to give up so easily. "It's a part of me," I said. "I've made it part of my story."

"Well then," she replied, "you should put it in your book."

My girlfriend was more understanding.

"Nice one," she said, and it was.

Nine days after the puzzle appeared in the *Guardian*, a list of the winners appeared. I called them all, to see what they thought of it. Three couldn't remember the puzzle. They send in ten or fifteen entries a week, and a puzzle is forgotten as soon as it is finished. Two thought it was great, but both immediately made self-deprecating jokes. "I think that of everything by Araucaria," said one. "He seems to me to be head and shoulders above the rest." "Isn't he lovely?" asked the other. "Everything he does is so witty." The former is twenty-two years old and studying mathematics. The latter is seventy-six and has been doing crosswords for more than half a century. It seemed to me entirely appropriate that this puzzle should have brought pleasure to people so different in age.

Talking to these setters and solvers, however, I realize that I still have some way to go before my range of reference points equals theirs. I look forward to the journey.

It should be fun.

You could say the same of crosswords.[28]

prize
puzzle 22445

From the *Guardian*, February 16, 2002

Across

1 Here is Grub Street: writer's about (6)
4 Miss Elizabeth Hill on-line, says... (6)
9 ...Breck, concluding 21's name (4)
10 Having fun qualified for chastisement (10)
11 Tony transfigured and translated? Wait for it! (3,3)
12 It's very exciting when the stream enters the river (8)
13 Actor Matthew was mounted—a splendid chap outside (9)
15,17 Topiary —a bough damaged—story of my life! (13)
16 Actors are like flies (4)
17 See 15
21 Bird on the wing captivating American storyteller (8)
22 Put on to fool both of us, so to speak? (6)
24 Fancied filly gets to fling rider off... (10)
25 ...but he will win her love,... (4)
26 ...I forgot to mention, in heart and body (6)
27 English points of view (6)

Down

1 21's David's a degree over 54 (7)
2 Little boy that hasn't got shingles? (5)
3 Judge could be true defence counsel, perhaps (7)
5 I left the country before the fighter came in (6)
6 With family backing I commend a racing driver (4,5)
7 Put spirit into fruit (7)
8 Pompey's partner keeps crockery in place of junk (5,5,3)
14 Scotchman not moving between princess and mother-in-law (9)
16 Aid to detection said to turn up murderer— could be St Bernard (7)
18 Information about 9 to warm the heart (7)
19 It isn't so funny to be given the elbow (7)
20 One man in a boat on the Tweed? (6)
23 Revolutionary hales from Africa (5)

solution to

puzzle 22445

postscript

By rights, the last word should belong to Araucaria. Here it is. "How to keep up your reading? Happily, if romantic (4,4)."*

---

*BOOK ENDS. Actually, he set this in the *Financial Times*, and therefore it appeared under his other pseudonym, Cinephile (October 24, 2001).

notes

1. *Fynbos* is the major vegetation type of the small botanical region known as the "Cape Floral Kingdom." Only five other floral kingdoms are recognized, and these cover huge areas, such as the whole of Australia and most of the Northern Hemisphere.
2. All crossword people have favorite clues, even those (like me) who claim they don't. These two came to me from John Perkin, a longtime editor of the *Guardian* crossword, but others have mentioned them as well. They are credited to the late Alec Robins, who set under the pseudonym of Custos for the *Guardian*.
3. Attributed to Araucaria.
4. Strictly for Nick Hornby fans: 4–1 against Crystal Palace. Alan Smith scored twice, and—to add insult to injury—the defenders Tony Adams and Lee Dixon each got one.
5. By Araucaria, in the *Guardian*, September 5, 2001.
6. Bunthorne, in the *Guardian*, December 18, 2001.
7. Pasquale, in the *Guardian*, January 26, 2002.

8. Rover, in the *Guardian*, January 25, 2002.

9. Look Back in Anger . . . anKOOLger! by Paul, in the *Guardian*, March 23, 2002.

10. Victoria's double acrostic: a city in Italy; a River in Germany; a town in the United States; a town in North America; a town in Holland; the Turkish name for Constantinople; a town in Bothnia; a city in Greece; a circle on the globe.

11. By Audreus, in the *Guardian*, November 30, 2001.

12. A vote on whether or not to go ahead with the so-called "tri-cameral parliament." Such votes were normally boycotted by the white left, but in this case the referendum was notable for creating a momentary "NO" alliance between the left and the far right. As the veteran campaigner Helen Joseph put it, it was "only a one-night stand." Only people classified "white" voted in this referendum, and the apartheid government duly got its "yes."

13. By Chifonie, in the *Guardian*, January 11, 2002.

14. Yet another setter called *John*. Through a gradual, possibly inadvertent, culling, almost all *Guardian* setters appear now to be called *John*. Four of them got together to form Biggles, and occasional puzzles appear under that byline. Biggles was—of course—created by W. E. Johns, or as they put it, "we Johns."

15. Adrian Bell, foreword to the *Penguin Book of the Times 50th Anniversary Crosswords*, 1980, p. 10.

16. Don Manley, *Chambers Crossword Manual*, 2nd ed., 1992 (now in its 4th ed.).

17. Quoted in ibid, p. 59.

18. D. S. MacNutt, *Ximenes on the Art of the Crossword*, Methuen, 1966.

19. By Gemini, the *Guardian*, October 17, 2001.

20. James C. Scott, *Seeing Like a State: How Certain Schemes to Improve the Human Condition Have Failed*, Yale University Press, 1998, p. 357.

21. His full name was Robert Lewis Balfour Stevenson. The French spelling of "Louis" was an author's affectation, and "Balfour" was dropped altogether.

22. By Rover, August 9, 2001.

23. In the *Guardian*, September 11, 2000.

24. Scott, *op cit.* p. 357.

25. In a piece in the *Guardian* written by David McKie to commemorate Araucaria's eightieth birthday, this story is told the other way around, with "chaste" and "Archer" coming first. Araucaria claims not to remember. Either way, the story works.

26. Manley, *Chambers Crossword Manual,* p. 275.

27. *Guardian,* June 7, 2002.

28. It is worth noting that the first word in Arthur Wynne's first published crossword puzzle was FUN.

acknowledgments

I want to thank the many people who gave so freely of their time and their knowledge while I wrote this book. In particular, these crossword editors: Brian Greer and John Grant (both formerly of the *Times*), Mike Laws (the *Times*), Michael Mac-Donald Cooper (the *Independent* and *Independent on Sunday*), Don Manley (*Church Times*), the late John Perkin (formerly of the *Guardian*), Hugh Stephenson (the *Guardian*), and Will Shortz (the *New York Times*); and these crossword setters: Azed, Bunthorne, Cyclops, Enigmatist, Hornblower, Pasquale, Paul, Rufus, Shed, and Spurius. I also want to thank the many friends and colleagues whose ideas and critiques were invaluable in shaping this book, especially Andy Abrahams, Andrew Bethell, Graham Wickham, and Louise Swan. I am grateful to them all. I am especially indebted to my agent, Isobel Dixon, and to my editors, Toby Mundy and Wendy Hubbert.

There are two people for whom thanks are not enough: Araucaria, without whom there would be no puzzle, and my girlfriend, without whom there would be no story.

about
the
author

SANDY BALFOUR is an award-winning television journalist who has written, produced, and directed programs for CNN, the Discovery channel, and the BBC. Born in Johannesburg, Balfour now lives in London.